outdoor food

YOU

outdoor food

carmen niehaus

List of acknowledgements

Publishing a book is not a one-man project, since it requires the efforts of a great many people to ensure its success. I am much indebted to the guest cooks from all over who not only welcomed us into their establishments but willingly shared their recipes with us. Of course, no cookbook is complete without attractive photos – these frequently determine whether someone buys a book or not. I am very grateful to all the photographers who collaborated with me on these wonderful stories. I would also like to thank my former assistants, Arina du Plessis and Michelle Greyling of *Huisgenoot*, who tested recipes and developed some of them; Magda Herbst for typing the recipes; Anita Pyke of Human & Rousseau for coordinating the project; Annelene van der Merwe for editing the manuscript and Lindie Metz for the stunning lay-out of the book.

Guest cooks

Voorstrandt Restaurant, Paternoster , Tel. 022-752-2038
Caterer Pauline Schreuder of Moorreesburg, Tel. 082-494-6307
Caterer Adéle Wessels of Heidelberg (Cape), Tel. 028-722-2707
Caterer Marlene Swart of Stanford , Tel. 028-341-0929
Caterer Christine Capendale of Langebaan, Tel. 022-772-1086
Cookbook author Anne Meyers of Cape Town, Tel. 021-913-0799
Restaurant owner Hetta van Deventer of Laborie Restaurant, Paarl, Tel. 021-807-3095
Tritonia Coffee Shop, Heidelberg, Tel. 028-713-2557
Rooi Aalwyn Roadstall, Riversdale, Tel. 028-713-2237
Sanbona Wildlife Reserve, Barrydale , Tel. 028-572-1482
Interior designer and lifestyle guru David Strauss of David Strauss Interiors, Tel. 021-554-2283
Food expert and author Errieda du Toit of Errieda du Toit PR, Tel. 021-913-2248
SA food evangelist Francois Ferreira, chief of Eden Hospitality Service & Training Unit, Tel. 044-272-3653
Product range owner Tracy Foulkes of NoMU Brands (Pty) Ltd , http://www.nomu.co.za, Tel. 021-386-2000

Photo credits

Jacques Stander pp. 6, 8, 11, 14, 17, 18, 27, 122, 124, 127, 128, 136, 138, 144, 146, 147, 149, 150, 154, 155,
David Briers pp. 1, 9, 13, 20, 23, 25, 26, 28, 30, 33, 34, 35, 36, 37, 38, 41, 42, 43, 44, 46, 49, 50, 52, 53, 54, 56, 59, 60, 62, 63, 64, 66, 70, 72, 73, 74, 77, 79, 81, 82, 89, 90, 93, 95, 100, 102, 105, 108, 110, 111, 113, 114, 115, 116, 119, 130, 132, 135, 156, 159, 160, 163, 164, 166, 169, 170, 172, 173, 174, 177, 178, 181, 182, 184, 187
Dawie Verwey pp. 84, 87, 88
Neville Lockhart pp. 96, 99,
Adriaan Oosthuisen p. 142

First published in 2004 by Human & Rousseau
40 Heerengracht, Cape Town

10 9 8 7 6 5 4 3 2 1

Publisher	Anita Pyke
Editor	Annelene van der Merwe
Design and Typesetting	Lindie Metz
Food stylist	Carmen Niehaus

Reproduction by Cape Imaging Bureau, Cape Town
Printed in China through Colorcraft Ltd., Hong Kong

ISBN 0 7981 444 2 4

contents

communing

with nature

Discover the delights of nature by going on a safari – it could be to the Bushveld, Kalahari, the mountains or any place out of town. Gather around the campfire with a steaming pot of coffee, discuss the day and listen to the far-off calls of jackals to their mates; explore narrow footpaths and clamber over rugged cliffs; let the children run free and ask them to braai their own skewered bread over the coals; revel in the beauty of the landscape and allow it to bring peace to your soul.

on safari

The 4x4 is packed and you're ready to head for the great outdoors. No matter where you set up camp, everyone is in the mood for hearty campfire fare.

campfire popcorn

Campfire popcorn

Heat a little oil in a three-legged pot or a smaller pot placed over the fire on a stand. Sprinkle a single layer of popcorn in the pot and cover. Heat and leave the corn to pop, shaking the pot occasionally. When the popping has stopped remove the pot from the heat and season the popcorn with flavoured salt or Parmesan cheese.

Hint
For sweet popcorn, sprinkle with icing sugar.

Stuffed lamb chops

4–6 anchovies
30 ml (2 T) finely chopped
  parsley
2–4 garlic cloves
15 ml (1 T) balsamic vinegar
olive oil
8 lamb loin chops
salt and pepper

Serve these stuffed chops with Italian bean salad (see recipe on page 10).

Mash the anchovies, parsley, garlic, balsamic vinegar and enough olive oil to form a thick paste. Bone and trim the chops (you'll be left with a piece of meat that's almost kidney-shaped). Spoon the anchovy mixture into the hollow of each piece of meat, then bring the thinner end of the chop around the filling and over the thicker part to form a round. Secure with a cocktail stick. Season and braai over medium coals until done.
  Serves 4–6.

Pork chops with spinach and Parmesan cheese filling

8 thick pork chops
½ onion, grated
2 garlic cloves, crushed
olive oil
1 packet (500 g) frozen
  spinach
100 ml grated Parmesan
  cheese
salt and freshly ground
  black pepper

Make an incision in the meaty part of each chop right up to the bone to form a pocket. Stir-fry the onion and garlic in a little heated olive oil until tender. Add the spinach and stir-fry until all the moisture has evaporated. Remove from the heat and add the Parmesan cheese. Season to taste with salt and freshly ground black pepper. Spoon a little of the filling into each pocket and secure with a cocktail stick. Brush the chops with olive oil and season with salt and pepper. Braai over medium-hot coals until done and serve with pan bread and coarse hummus (see recipes on page 12).
  Serves 4–8.

Italian bean salad

1 small onion, finely chopped
1 stalk celery, finely chopped
1 red chilli, seeded and
  chopped
10 ml (2 t) chopped fresh
  oregano
1 can (410 g) each butter
  beans, sugar beans and red
  kidney beans, drained
6 ripe tomatoes, seeded
  and chopped
45 ml (3 T) chopped fresh
  parsley
juice of 1 lemon
salt and freshly ground
  black pepper

dressing
60 ml (4 T) olive oil
45 ml (3 T) lemon juice
salt and black pepper

Mix all the salad ingredients and season to taste with salt and pepper. Blend the ingredients for the dressing and pour over the salad. Stand for at least 2 hours to allow the flavours to develop.

Serves 4–6.

Potato salad

6 large potatoes
juice of ½ lemon
60 ml (4 T) olive oil
15 ml (1 T) dried basil
salt and freshly ground
  black pepper
1 small onion, chopped
12 pitted green olives, halved
5 gherkins, chopped
5 plum tomatoes, seeded and
  roughly chopped
4 hard-boiled eggs

Serve this filling potato salad for lunch while camping. It can even be made the day before and simply taken along if you move camp.

Cook the potatoes in their jackets in salted water until tender. Drain and cube without removing the skins. Whisk the lemon juice and oil together, add the basil and salt and pepper to taste and pour over the hot potatoes. Set aside to cool. Add the remaining ingredients except the eggs. Shell the eggs just before serving and cut into pieces or chop roughly. Add to the salad and mix lightly. Serve with pan bread (see recipe on page 12) if desired.

Serves 6.

potato salad

Pan bread

dough
1 packet (500 g) self-raising
  flour
5 ml (1 t) salt
20 ml (4 t) sugar
½ packet (7 ml) instant yeast
30 ml (2 T) oil
300 ml lukewarm water

Enjoy chunks of this bread with a coarse hummus, instantly made with a can of chickpeas. Use the same dough to prepare the pan pizza.

Combine the self-raising flour, salt and sugar and sprinkle the instant yeast on top. Pour the oil and lukewarm water over the flour mixture and mix to form a stiff dough. Knead until smooth and elastic and the dough no longer sticks to your hands. Cover and leave to rise until doubled in volume. Knock down and divide the dough into 12 uniform balls. Flatten them slightly and leave to rise once more until doubled in volume. Heat a pan and grease with a little oil. Place a few of the balls of dough in the pan at a time and cook, turning occasionally, until brown on the outside and cooked inside. The bread is done when it sounds hollow when tapped. Serve with hummus and olive oil.
  Makes 12.

Hints

- Make sure that you include a can of Egyptian dukkah to your camping list when you go camping. Serve the pan bread as a starter before the meal. Place the bread with little bowls of dukkah and olive oil on a tray and enjoy by firstly dipping the bread in the oil and then in the dukkah.
- Cut any leftover bread in half, braai over the coals and serve for breakfast with butter and jam.

Coarse hummus

Drain 1 can (400 g) chickpeas and mash with a fork to form a coarse paste. Season with olive oil, the juice of half a lemon, salt and pepper and add a handful of sesame seeds. Serve with pan bread.
  Makes about 500 ml (2 c).

Couscous pudding

300 ml milk
60 ml (4 T) sugar
40 ml butter
1 cinnamon stick
2 star anise
few strips orange rind
300 ml couscous
100 g (½ packet) mixed nuts,
    toasted and chopped
125 g pitted dates, chopped

Couscous is really versatile – use it to make side dishes, salads or puddings.

Bring the milk, sugar, butter, spices and orange rind to the boil. Pour the milk mixture over the couscous, cover and leave to stand until the couscous has plumped out. Stir in the nuts and dates. Serve with thin custard or cream.
    Serves 4.

Naartjie pudding

sauce
500 ml (2 c) naartjie or orange
    pulp, including rind
150 ml water
375 ml (1½ c) sugar

batter
60 ml (4 T) melted butter
125 ml (½ c) milk
1 egg, whisked
375 ml (1½ c) cake flour
12,5 ml (2½ t) baking powder
pinch salt
125 ml (½ c) sugar

Prepare the sauce beforehand and keep in a bottle.

Make the sauce by combining the ingredients and bring to the boil.
    Grease a cast-iron pot and pour in the sauce. To make the batter combine the butter, milk and egg. Sift the dry ingredients together, add the sugar and fold into the egg mixture. Spoon the batter on top of the sauce in the pot. Cover and cook over medium coals for 10–15 minutes. Serve with ice cream mixed with toasted almonds.

naartjie pudding

Bobotie in a cast-iron pot

375 ml (1½ c) brown lentils,
  rinsed
salt to taste
2 slices bread, crusts
  removed
150 ml water or milk
500 ml (2 c) dried mince
  (see recipe)
2 onions, sliced into rings
2 garlic cloves, crushed
oil
15 ml (1 T) mild curry powder
5 ml (1 t) turmeric
5 ml (1 t) ground coriander
3 ml (generous ½ t) cumin
45 ml (3 T) white grape
  vinegar
60 ml (4 T) chutney
15 ml (1 T) Worcester sauce
7 ml (1½ t) salt
freshly ground black pepper
60 ml (4 T) seedless raisins

topping
3 eggs
180 ml (¾ c) milk

We made this bobotie with dried mince and lentils. Cook it in a cast-iron pot over the fire.

Cook the lentils in water until tender. Season to taste. Drain and set aside. Soak the bread in the water or milk and set aside. Hydrate the mince as described in the recipe on page 16 and set aside for a few minutes to let it absorb the moisture. Meanwhile fry the onions and garlic in heated oil in a flat-bottomed pot until soft. Add the spices and stir-fry until fragrant. Add the mince and fry until just done. Add the remaining ingredients, including the lentils and bread. Simmer for a few minutes, then smooth the top until level.

Topping: Beat the eggs and milk and pour over the mince mixture. Cover and place a few coals on the lid. Leave for about 10 minutes or until the egg mixture has set and is cooked. Serve with extra chutney and rice.

Serves 6–8.

Pan pizza

dough
1 packet (500 g) self-raising
  flour
5 ml (1 t) salt
20 ml (4 t) sugar
7 ml (½ packet) instant yeast
30 ml (2 T) oil
300 ml lukewarm water

topping
basil pesto
anchovies
fried bacon
salami
piquanté peppers
gherkins
canned pineapple
olives
mozzarella cheese

Invest in a black potjie with a flat lid – it's ideal for making this pizza.

Combine the self-raising flour, salt and sugar and sprinkle the instant yeast on top. Pour the oil and lukewarm water over the flour mixture and mix to form a stiff dough. Knead until smooth and elastic and the dough no longer sticks to your hands. Cover and leave to rise until doubled in volume. Knock down and shape the dough into a large flat round. Spray the griddle side of the flat lid of a black potjie with nonstick spray and place the dough on top. Leave to rise again. Place the lid on a tripod or a grid and heat over the fire until the dough is just done. Turn so the browned side is on top. Spread with a layer of basil pesto and arrange the topping ingredients on top. Sprinkle with cubes of mozzarella cheese. Place an upturned pot or a lid over the pizza and place a few coals on top. Heat until the cheese has melted and the topping ingredients are heated through.

Serves 4–6.

Boerewors with Moroccan couscous

1 onion, chopped
30 ml (2 T) butter
150 g raisins
30 ml (2 T) brown sugar
10 ml (2 t) grated fresh ginger
10 ml (2 t) ground cinnamon
5 ml (1 t) cumin
5 ml (1 t) ground coriander
500 ml (2 c) chicken stock
500 ml (2 c) couscous
100 g almonds, chopped
8–10 portion-size pieces
  boerewors

Sauté the onion in butter until soft. Add the raisins, brown sugar, ginger, cinnamon, cumin and coriander. Fry until the mixture begins to caramelise and set aside. Bring the chicken stock to the boil and pour over the couscous. Cover and leave for 10 minutes. Fluff up with a fork and stir in the almonds along with the onion mixture.

Braai the boerewors and serve with the couscous.

Serves 6–8.

Boerewors with polenta

750 ml (3 c) water
150 g polenta
3 ml (generous ½ t) salt
125 ml (½ c) grated
  Parmesan cheese
30 ml (2 T) chopped
  fresh parsley
45 ml (3 T) olive oil
8 pieces of boerewors
45 ml (3 T) olive oil

Bring the water to the boil. Add the polenta and salt. Beat to prevent lumps forming. Simmer for 8–10 minutes. Remove from the heat and add grated Parmesan cheese, chopped fresh parsley and olive oil. Spoon into a 20 x 20 cm baking pan and leave to cool. When firm, cut into 8 wedges. Braai the boerewors over medium-hot coals until done. Brush the polenta wedges with olive oil and braai over the fire until golden brown. Serve with the boerewors.

Serves 6–8.

Dried mince

This is a must, especially if your cold storage is limited. YOU photographer Jacques Stander says he often uses it when he goes camping in Malawi.

Preheat the oven to 100 °C (200 °F). Season lean mince with salt and pepper only. Fry in a heated pan without oil until cooked and all the moisture has evaporated. Spoon a thin layer of the mince on baking sheets, spreading evenly. Place the mince in the oven for 3–4 hours until dry but not burnt. Stir occasionally. Leave to cool before vacuum-packing or storing in an airtight container.

To cook the mince, add 250–375 ml (1–1½ c) boiling water to every 250 ml (1 c) dried mince and leave until hydrated. Season the meat to taste and use to make pasta dishes, meat fillings for vetkoek or pancakes, pies or bobotie.

1 kg (4 c) raw mince makes 500 ml (2 c) dried mince.

Nut bars

500 ml (2 c) oats
125 ml (½ c) desiccated
  coconut
150 g butter
50 ml brown sugar
75 ml (5 T) golden syrup
50 g (½ packet) blanched
  almonds, chopped
100 g (1 packet) Brazil or
  cashew nuts
80 g dark chocolate,
  broken into squares
  and finely chopped

These bars, rich in energy, fibre and nuts, make delicious snacks to take along on a camping trip.

Preheat the oven to 180 °C (350 °F) and grease a baking sheet with butter or margarine or spray with nonstick spray.

Combine the oats and coconut in a bowl and set aside. Heat the butter, sugar and syrup over low heat until the sugar has dissolved, stirring occasionally. Remove from the heat and stir in the oats mixture. Spoon onto the prepared baking sheet and press down firmly. Sprinkle the nuts and chocolate on top, pressing them slightly into the bottom layer. Bake for 30 minutes until light golden brown. Cut into bars while still lukewarm. Allow to cool and store in an airtight container.

Makes 30 bars.

boerewors with polenta

campfire cooking

Break away from it all and enjoy a weekend out in the open. Use these recipes for a weekend's worth of meals you can cook over the fire or in a pot.

Friday supper
Lamb kebab curry with
  skewered bread

Saturday breakfast
Mock must rusks
  with coffee

Lunch
Breyani potjie with
  tomato sambal

Potjiekos supper
Lamb shank potjie with
  savoury mealie meal
  porridge
Vegetable potjie

Sunday brunch
Creamy Maltabella
  porridge
Potato cake with
  feta spread

Sunday braai
Butterflied chicken over
  the coals
Vegetable parcels
Chocolate fondue with
  marshmallows

Supper
Pork stir-fry with couscous

Lamb kebab curry

1 kg cubed lamb
8 cm piece fresh ginger,
  peeled and thinly sliced
8-12 pickling onions
olive oil
1 small onion, peeled
  and chopped
6-8 garlic cloves, crushed
4 chillies
60 ml (4 T) curry powder
50 ml tomato purée
250 ml (1 c) hot chicken stock
lemon juice
salt and freshly ground
  black pepper

Thread the meat cubes, ginger slices and pickling onions on 6 kebab skewers (cut the skewers slightly shorter to fit in the bottom of your pot). Set aside.

Heat a little olive oil in a flat cast-iron pot. Sauté the chopped onion, garlic and chillies until soft and fragrant. Sprinkle the curry powder over and stir-fry for about a minute longer. Add the tomato purée and half the stock and bring to the boil. Add the meat kebabs, cover and simmer slowly until the meat is tender and done. Add more stock as needed. Season with a little lemon juice, salt and freshly ground pepper to taste.

Serve with skewered bread (see recipe below) or with rice.
Serves 4–6.

Easy skewered bread

300 ml (1¼ c) beer
50 g butter
60 ml (4 T) brown sugar
1 egg, whisked
500 ml (2 c) white bread flour
500 ml (2 c) cake flour
12 ml (2½ t) instant yeast
5 ml (1 t) salt

Bring the beer, butter and sugar to the boil and remove from the heat. Cool until lukewarm. Beat in the egg. In a large bowl combine the flours, yeast and salt and make a well in the centre. Pour the beer mixture into the well and mix to form a soft dough. Knead the dough until smooth and elastic. Place the dough in an oiled bowl, cover with clingwrap or a cloth and leave in a warm place to rise until doubled in volume.

Knock down and divide into 8 equal pieces. Roll each piece of dough into a long, thin sausage. Wrap one end of the dough around a long skewer and twist the rest of the dough sausage around the skewer in a spiral, leaving enough room at the bottom of the skewer to hold it while toasting the bread. Hold the skewered bread over cool coals, turning regularly until done, about 12–15 minutes.

Serve with apricot jam and the lamb kebab curry (see recipe above).
Makes 8.

Hint
After supper, use the skewers for toasting marshmallows.

Mock must rusks

1 kg cake flour
5 ml (1 t) salt
125 ml (½ c) sugar
2 packets (10 g each) instant
  yeast
45 ml (3 T) aniseed
¾ can condensed milk
about 500 ml (2 c) lukewarm
  water
200 g butter or margarine,
  melted

Bake the rusks at home and serve with coffee for breakfast.

Sift together the flour and salt and mix with the sugar, instant yeast and aniseed. Add the condensed milk and just enough water to form a dough. Knead well, adding just enough of the remaining water to form a soft dough. Regularly grease your hands with the melted butter or margarine. Knead the dough for about 15–20 minutes or until smooth and elastic. Spread the remaining melted butter or margarine over the dough, cover and leave to rise in a warm place until doubled in volume. Knock down gently and shape into balls. Arrange the balls in 3–4 greased loaf tins, cover and leave to rise again until doubled in volume.

Meanwhile, preheat the oven to 180 °C (350 °F) and bake the rusks for 1 hour or until done and golden brown on top. Leave to cool, break into pieces and dry in a cool oven at 100 °C (200 °F).

Makes 3 dozen large rusks.

mock must rusks

Breyani potjie

marinade
15 ml (1 T) oil
250 ml (1 c) buttermilk
10 ml (2 t) red masala
7 ml (1½ t) turmeric
5 ml (1 t) ground cinnamon
10 ml (2 t) ground coriander
10 ml (2 t) ground cumin
1–2 green chillies, seeded
  and finely chopped
2 garlic cloves, crushed
2 cm piece fresh ginger,
  grated
1 can (400 g) chopped
  tomatoes

breyani
1,5 kg chicken pieces,
  skinned and boned
675 ml (2¾ c) uncooked rice
3 ml (generous ½ t) turmeric
4 cinnamon sticks
4 cardamom pods
salt
500 ml (2 c) brown lentils
30 ml (2 T) oil
2 onions, thinly sliced
4 potatoes, peeled and
  thinly sliced
125 ml (½ c) chicken stock

Mix all the ingredients for the marinade. Place the chicken pieces in a nonmetallic bowl, pour the marinade over, cover and chill for at least 2 hours.

Meanwhile cook the rice with the turmeric, cinnamon sticks, cardamom pods and salt until done. Drain. Cook the lentils in salted water until soft, only adding salt towards the end of the cooking period. Drain and set aside along with the rice.

Heat the 30 ml (2 T) oil in a large cast-iron pot and fry the onions until soft. Add the potatoes and fry until golden brown. Add the chicken pieces and marinade, fry until the meat is lightly browned on the outside and simmer until done.

Remove the chicken pieces from the pot. Arrange alternating layers of chicken, rice mixture and lentils in the pot. Pour the stock over, cover and steam over very low heat until fragrant, about 30 minutes.

Serve with a cucumber yoghurt sauce and tomato and onion sambal.

Serves 6–8.

How to prepare cucumber yoghurt sauce
Cube a quarter of a cucumber and mix with plain yoghurt. Season with a pinch of cumin.

Lamb shank potjie

2 kg lamb shanks, cut into
  long pieces
salt and freshly ground
  black pepper
30 ml (2 T) butter
30 ml (2 T) olive oil
2 onions, chopped
4 celery stalks, chopped
30 ml (2 T) cake flour
250–500 ml (1–2 c) dry
  white wine
500 ml (2 c) chicken stock
125 ml (½ c) chopped
  fresh parsley
10 ml (2 t) dried oregano
60 ml (4 T) lemon juice
3 egg yolks

Season the shanks well with salt and pepper. Heat the butter and oil in a cast-iron pot and brown the shanks. Remove from the pot and set aside. In the same pot, sauté the onions and celery until soft. Add the cake flour and heat for a few minutes, stirring continuously. Add 250 ml (1 c) of the white wine, bring to the boil and cook until the liquid has reduced by half. Add the stock, parsley and oregano. Return the meat to the pot, cover and simmer slowly for 2½ hours or until the meat is tender (add more white wine if the pot seems dry). Remove the meat from the pot. Beat the lemon juice and egg yolks with 125 ml (½ c) of the meat sauce. Remove the pot from the heat and stir the egg yolk mixture into the sauce. Return the meat to the pot and mix.

Serve with savoury mealie meal porridge.

Serves 6.

Savoury mealie meal porridge

1–1,5 litres (4–6 c) water
10 ml (2 t) olive oil
25 ml (5 t) butter
salt
3 garlic cloves, peeled
3 sprigs thyme
500 g mealie meal
finely chopped fresh parsley
butter

Combine the water, oil, butter, salt, garlic and thyme in a large pot and bring to the boil. Sprinkle the mealie meal on top, stirring continuously. Cover and simmer slowly for about 1 hour, stirring occasionally. Stir in parsley and butter to taste and serve with Lamb shank potjie (see recipe on previous page).

Vegetable potjie

oil
1 onion, sliced
3 garlic cloves, crushed
1 large cabbage, cut
  into slices
1 cauliflower, broken
  into florets
salt and pepper
grated nutmeg
200 g feta cheese, crumbled
6–8 sun-dried tomatoes in
  vinaigrette, chopped
butter
balsamic vinegar

Heat a little oil in a pot, add the onion and garlic and stir-fry until glossy. Add the cabbage and cauliflower, season to taste with salt, pepper and nutmeg. Cover and heat until the vegetables are just done. Add water if necessary. Sprinkle with feta cheese and tomatoes, mix lightly and heat until the cheese has just melted. Dot with butter, mix through and serve with a dash of balsamic vinegar.
  Serves 6.

Creamy Maltabella porridge

Cook the porridge according to the packet instructions. Season with brown sugar and cinnamon and serve with luke-warm cream, flavoured with a little vanilla essence.

vegetable potjie

Potato cake

6 eggs, lightly whisked
250 ml (1 c) milk
60 ml (4 T) olive oil
250 ml (1 c) cake flour
3 potatoes, peeled
　and grated
2 onions, grated
150 g spinach, washed,
　hard stems removed,
　and shredded
30 ml (2 T) chopped
　fresh thyme
salt and freshly ground
　black pepper
oil for frying

This dish can also be prepared in a skottelbraai.

Beat the eggs, milk and olive oil together. Sift the flour and slowly stir in the egg mixture to form a smooth batter. Add the potatoes, onions, spinach and thyme and season well with salt and black pepper. Heat a little oil in a large pan and pour the mixture into the pan or skottelbraai. Cook high above cool coals until set underneath. Cover the cake with a sheet of foil and arrange a few coals on top of the foil. Continue heating until the cake is slightly browned on top and completely set, about 15–20 minutes, depending on the size of the pan and the heat of the coals.

　Serve with feta cheese spread (see recipe below).
　Serves 4–6.

Feta spread

300 g feta cheese
300 ml thick plain yoghurt
2 garlic cloves, crushed
5 ml (1 t) paprika
2 ml (½ t) cayenne pepper
salt and freshly ground black
　pepper to taste
15 ml (1 T) olive oil

Make in advance and chill.

Process the feta cheese and yoghurt until smooth. Add the garlic, paprika, cayenne pepper, salt and freshly ground black pepper to taste. Drizzle with the olive oil and chill until needed. Serve with the potato cake.

　Makes 500 ml (2 c) spread.

Butterflied chicken over the coals

marinade
125 ml (½ c) lemon juice
80 ml (⅓ c) honey
45-60 ml (3-4 T) sweet
　chilli sauce
3-4 cloves garlic, crushed
　(optional)

chicken
2 whole chickens
salt and freshly ground
　black pepper
olive oil

Add up to 125 ml (½ c) honey if you don't use sweet chilli sauce in the marinade.

Mix all the ingredients for the marinade. Butterfly the chickens by cutting along the breastbone with a sharp knife and splaying open. Brush the chickens with the spice mixture, cover and chill overnight. Leave the chickens outside to reach room temperature before cooking.

　Secure in a folding braai grid and braai over medium coals until the skin is crisp and the juices run clear when the meat is pricked in the thickest part with a skewer. Season with salt and pepper and drizzle with olive oil.

　Serve with plain yoghurt seasoned with garlic, salt and pepper, as well as vegetable parcels (see recipe on next page).
　Serves 6–8.

Vegetable parcels

Prepare a variety of vegetables, cut them into bite-size pieces and arrange on a few sheets of foil. Prepare a selection of flavoured butters by mixing butter with seasonings such as cumin, chilli, thyme, rosemary, flavoured salt and garlic. Dot the vegetables with a butter of your choice and wrap in the foil. Braai over hot coals until done.

butterflied chicken over the coals, with vegetable parcels

Chocolate fondue with marshmallows

In a small black pot, slowly heat 200 g chocolate, broken into squares, with 250 ml (1 c) cream. Stir continuously until the chocolate has melted. Dip marshmallows threaded onto skewers in the chocolate sauce.

Pork stir-fry

marinade
20 ml (4 t) curry powder
60 ml (4 T) fish sauce
60 ml (4 T) lemon juice
20 ml (4 t) brown sugar
20 ml (4 t) cornflour
250 ml (2 c) water

stir-fry
1,5 kg pork strips
60 ml (4 T) oil
2-3 red chillies, seeded and chopped
12 spring onions, chopped
100 g (1 packet) unsalted cashew nuts
salt and freshly ground black pepper

Enjoy as a light meal.

Mix all the ingredients for the marinade. Pour over the pork strips. Heat the oil in a skottelbraai or wok. When very hot, remove the pork strips from the marinade and stir-fry along with the chillies and spring onions until browned. Add the remaining marinade and heat until slightly thickened and cooked. Add the cashew nuts and season to taste with salt and freshly ground black pepper.
   Serve with rice or couscous and a mixed salad.
   Serves 4–6.

Camp catering

Here's a list of suggested foods to take on safari.

- Savoury instant rice, pasta, couscous, polenta or braai pap, lentils
- Canned food such as tomatoes (different flavours), chickpeas, tomato and onion mix, beans and whole-kernel corn, canned pineapple, piquanté peppers, gherkins, olives, tuna, anchovies, mixed nuts and dried fruit
- Sachets of tomato paste, basil and sun-dried tomato pesto, chutney and sauces
- Various types of flavoured salts, braai salt, spices, red and green curry paste or a good curry mixture, coconut milk powder, freeze-dried Parmesan cheese, nonstick cooking spray, olive oil and balsamic vinegar
- Instant bread and cake mixes, custard, Creamo, long-life milk and cream
- Packets of fresh herbs
- Fresh vegetables such as butternut, carrots, beetroot, potatoes, onions and garlic, plum tomatoes (they last longer than ordinary tomatoes), lemons and oranges
- Mozzarella lasts longer than Cheddar or Gouda because of a lower fat content
- Vacuum-packed chops and whole meat cuts

relaxing at the seaside

Revel in the bracing sea air and the murmur of the waves; enjoy the feel of sea sand between your toes and the sun caressing your bare skin. Watch toddlers building sand castles and people playing beach tennis or surfing in the waves, but be sure to check the coals occasionally to see whether they are ready for a fresh catch. At dusk the scene changes, when an elegantly set table above the high-water mark offers privileged diners delights such as mussel soup, seafood curry and even lamb shanks with caramelised onions, followed by brandy snaps for dessert.

seafood feast – West Coast style

At Paternoster on the West Coast there's a green and red corrugated iron shack right on the beach. Sometimes the tide comes to the foot of the stairs and you feel you could almost touch the whales in the bay. This is the Voorstrandt Restaurant where the food is served fresh from the sea. Fish and chips never tasted this good.

mussel soup

Menu

Mussel soup
Garlic mussels
Angelfish spread

Malay seafood curry
Marinated vegetable salad

Fruit flambé
Chocolate pecan pie

Mussel soup

3 tomatoes, peeled
1 onion, chopped
1 celery stalk, chopped
1 garlic clove
1 can (100 g) smoked mussels
  in oil
fresh or dried basil
1 vegetable stock cube
250 ml (1 c) cream
250 ml (1 c) milk
1 packet (50 g) white sauce
  powder, blended with a
  little milk
250 g cooked fresh mussels,
  shelled
12 cooked fresh mussels in
  their shells
salt and freshly ground
  black pepper

Process the tomatoes, onion, celery, garlic and smoked mussels (with the oil) in a food processor until smooth. Season to taste with basil. In a saucepan, dissolve the vegetable stock cube in 1 litre boiling water and add the smoked mussel mixture, cream and milk. Bring to the boil and thicken with the white sauce powder mixture. Add the fresh mussels and heat until the soup just comes to the boil. Remove from the heat and season to taste with salt and pepper. Serve with freshly baked bread.
   Serves 6–8.

Garlic mussels

6 fresh cooked or frozen
  mussels on the half shell
6 brown bread fingers
3–4 garlic cloves, finely
  chopped
125 ml (½ c) butter

Immerse the mussels in hot water for 5 minutes. Arrange the mussels in a circle on a plate, alternating with the bread fingers. Heat the garlic and butter and when the butter has melted, pour it over the mussels and bread. Heat in the microwave for 30 seconds or until just warm. Serve immediately.
   Serves 1.

Angelfish spread

1 onion, chopped
125 g butter
freshly ground black pepper
  to taste
2 ml (½ t) grated nutmeg
500 g smoked angelfish,
  boned and flaked
250 ml (1 c) cream

This spread freezes well.

In a fairly deep saucepan, stir-fry the onion in the butter until soft. Season with black pepper and nutmeg. Add the angelfish and cream. Bring to the boil, then process in a food processor until smooth. Chill. Serve with toast triangles and pickles such as gherkins, onions and piquanté peppers.
   Serves 14–16 as a starter or snack.

Malay seafood curry

50 ml sunflower oil
10 ml (2 t) mild curry powder
600 g frozen seafood mixture
  (marinara)
100 g frozen crabsticks, cut
  into pieces
12 cooked fresh mussels
2 cans (400 g each) Indian
  chopped tomatoes
25 ml (5 t) sugar

Heat the oil in a saucepan and fry the curry powder until fragrant. Add the remaining ingredients, mix, reduce the heat, cover and simmer for about 10 minutes or until fragrant. Serve with basmati rice, desiccated coconut, chutney, banana, plain yoghurt mixed with a little grated cucumber, and poppadums.

Serves 3–4.

Marinated vegetable salad

1 kg fresh vegetables such as
  cauliflower, broccoli, sweet
  peppers, baby marrows, red
  cabbage, mushrooms and
  baby corn
50 ml olive oil
roast vegetable seasoning
  (available in packets) or
  flavoured sea salt
100 g feta cheese

Cut the vegetables into uniform chunks and place in a microwave-proof dish. Add the olive oil and sprinkle to taste with the seasoning. Microwave at 100 per cent power until the vegetables are just done but still slightly crisp – about 7 minutes, depending on the kind of vegetables. Stir occasionally. Leave to cool until lukewarm or at room temperature before crumbling the feta cheese on top. Serve with your favourite salad dressing.

Serves 4.

Fruit flambé

2 peaches
2 pears
2 red apples with peel, cored
2 kiwi fruit
2 mangoes
2 bananas
200 ml brown sugar
200 ml brandy

Slice the fruit into strips. Heat a saucepan, add the fruit and sprinkle with the sugar. Stir-fry the fruit until heated through but not mushy. Add the brandy and heat slightly. Ignite the sauce and shake the pan until the flame has died down. Serve with ice cream.

Serves 4–6.

Malay seafood curry

marinated vegetable salad

Chocolate pecan pie

crust
250 g cake flour
125 g cold butter, diced
50 ml icing sugar
1 egg yolk
50 ml ice-cold water

filling
250 ml (1 c) cocoa powder
25 ml (5 t) vanilla essence
1 can (410 g) evaporated milk
750 g soft brown sugar
4 extra-large eggs
50 ml melted butter
100 g pecan nuts

Preheat the oven to 180 °C (350 °F) and grease a 24–26 cm loose-bottomed pie tin or two 20 cm loose-bottomed pie tins well with butter or spray with nonstick spray.

Crust: Place all the ingredients in a food processor and pulse until the mixture forms a ball around the blade. Remove from the food processor, press the dough together and press into the pie tin. Prick the base of the crust all over. Chill.

Filling: Beat all the ingredients except the pecan nuts together and spoon into the prepared crust. Arrange pecan nut halves around the edge of the pie and crumble the rest on top. Place the pie on a low shelf in the oven and bake for 45 minutes or until the filling is cooked and set.

Leave to cool and serve lukewarm or cold with cream or ice cream.

Makes 1 large pie.

chocolate pecan pie

fish braai on the beach

Have a convivial beach braai with plenty of seafood, but first make sure that braaing is permitted in the spot you've chosen.

Menu

Potato wedges with garlic
   mayonnaise

Whole fish baked in foil
   with herb butter
Moroccan calamari with
   red pepper salsa
Mealies with garlic butter
Vegetable kebabs and
   griddle cakes

Tropical fruit platter

Potato wedges

4–6 large potatoes, unpeeled
olive oil spray
coarse salt

Delicious – prepare these wedges in advance and serve as a snack while the rest of the food is on the braai.

Scrub the potatoes well and place in enough cold salted water to cover. Bring to the boil and cook until tender. Drain, cool slightly and cut into wedges. Spray with olive oil and sprinkle with coarse salt. Braai over medium coals until crisp and golden brown. Serve with garlic mayonnaise (see recipe below).
   Serves 4–6.

Garlic mayonnaise

1 whole garlic bulb, top
   removed
30 ml (2 T) olive oil
90 ml (6 T) thick mayonnaise
juice of ½ lemon
salt and black pepper

Brush the garlic with the olive oil and wrap in aluminium foil. Grill over the coals or roast in a 190 °C (375 °F) oven for 30–40 minutes or until tender. Cool. Press out the cooked garlic purée and mix with the remaining ingredients. Season to taste and chill until needed.
   Serve with potato wedges (see recipe above).
   Makes about 125 ml (½ c).

potato wedges, garlic mayonnaise, mealies with garlic butter and vegetable kebabs

whole fish with garlic butter

Whole fish baked in foil

2 fairly large whole fish,
  scaled and gutted
2 chives, chopped
lemon wedges

herb butter
175 g soft butter
30 ml (2 T) fresh coriander
3 garlic cloves, crushed
7 ml (1½ t) ground cumin
  (jeera)
7 ml (1½ t) paprika
½ red chilli, seeded and
  finely chopped
finely grated rind of 1 lemon
salt and black pepper

*The fish is rubbed with a healthy knob of savoury herb butter.
The aluminium foil wrapping is ideal for the beach as it keeps
out the sand.*

Wash the fish under cold, running water and remove the fins.
Make 4 slashes on each side of both fish. Place each fish on
a double layer of aluminium foil. Mix together all the ingredients for the herb butter until well-blended. Rub the fish well
with the herb butter, ensuring the incisions are well-greased.
Sprinkle the fish with the chopped chives, wrap tightly in the
foil and braai over medium coals for about 15–20 minutes or
until done and the flesh is no longer glassy. Serve with lemon
wedges.
    Serves 4–6.

Moroccan calamari

30 ml (2 T) chopped
  fresh coriander
30 ml (2 T) chopped
  fresh parsley
4 garlic cloves, crushed
5 ml (1 t) paprika
2 ml (½ t) ground coriander
2 ml (½ t) ground cumin
2 ml (½ t) cayenne pepper
juice of ½ lemon
30 ml (2 T) olive oil
salt and freshly ground
  black pepper
10 calamari tubes, sliced
  open
20 kebab skewers, soaked in
  boiling water

Process the herbs, spices, lemon juice and olive oil in a food
processor to form a smooth paste. Season with salt and pepper. Marinate the calamari in the mixture for about 4 hours.
Open the tubes, remove any film and thread a kebab skewer
through each end of the open calamari tube as you'd tack a
needle through a piece of material. Braai over medium coals
until just done, taking care not to overcook them.
    Serve with red pepper salsa (see recipe below).
    Serves 4–6.

Red pepper salsa

3 red sweet peppers, seeded
  and halved
3 whole cloves garlic,
  unpeeled
45 ml (3 T) olive oil
15 ml (1 T) balsamic vinegar
salt and freshly ground
  black pepper

Braai the peppers and garlic cloves over the coals for 20 minutes or until soft and slightly charred on the outside. Place
the peppers in a plastic bag and seal to allow them to sweat.
When cool, remove the skins and chop the flesh. Squeeze
out the cooked garlic purée and add to the chopped peppers.
Mix in the olive oil and vinegar and season to taste with salt
and pepper. Serve with Moroccan calamari or with salad and
griddle cakes (see recipe on page 40).
    Makes about 200 ml.

Mealies with garlic butter

6 corn on the cob,
  leaves intact
115 g soft butter
2 cloves garlic, crushed
15 ml (1 T) chopped fresh
  coriander (optional)

I prefer boiling the mealies beforehand and braaiing them just before serving to impart a smoky flavour.

Loosen the leaves of the mealies without removing them from the cob. Remove the beard. Fold the leaves back and cook the mealies in rapidly boiling water until nearly tender. Mix the butter, garlic and fresh coriander (if used) and spread a thick layer over each mealie. Fold the leaves back over the cobs and secure with string. Grill over coals until lightly browned.
  Serves 6.

Vegetable kebabs

4 baby marrows, halved
  lengthways and sliced
  into chunks
2 tomatoes
wooden skewers soaked in
  salted water
olive oil spray
coarse salt

Enjoy these vegetable kebabs with garlic mayonnaise or place them inside opened griddle cakes with a generous dollop of garlic mayonnaise. Any vegetables can be used.

Using a sharp knife, make a cross in the fleshy side of each baby marrow half. Slice the tomatoes into wedges. Thread the vegetables onto the skewers, alternating them. Spray with olive oil and sprinkle with coarse salt. Braai over medium coals until just tender. Turn occasionally.
  Serves 4.

Griddle cakes

Buy bread dough at the supermarket and shape into small balls. Roll in extra flour and arrange on a baking sheet or in a plastic container and leave to rise. When nicely risen braai the cakes high above the coals until they're done and sound hollow when tapped. Turn frequently. Serve with vegetable kebabs and a dollop of garlic mayonnaise, or with butter and syrup.

Tropical fruit platter

ripe pawpaw
ripe pineapple, leaves intact
granadillas
strawberries, with stalks

Fresh fruit is the easiest dessert for a braai.

Slice the pawpaw and cut the pineapple into wedges, leaves and all. Halve the granadillas and leave the strawberries whole.

Variation
Thread fruit onto skewers, braai slightly over the coals and serve with maple syrup.

tropical fruit platter

beach banquet

Well-known caterer Pauline Schreuder of Moorreesburg enjoys serving meals in unusual surroundings. Join her for this sumptuous dinner on the beach at Ganzekraal on the Cape West Coast.

Menu
Breadsticks

Seafood platter

Lamb shanks with
  caramelised onions
Oven-roasted mealies and
  waterblommetjies
Baby potato and spinach
  salad

Brandy snaps with fruit

Breadsticks

250 g butter
1 ml (¼ t) salt
250 ml (1 c) sour cream
about 750 ml (3 c) cake flour
250 ml (1 c) grated
  Cheddar cheese

The dough will keep for 2–3 weeks in the fridge.

Preheat the oven to 200 °C (400 °F) and grease a baking sheet with butter or margarine or spray with nonstick spray.

Beat the butter and salt together with a wooden spoon. Gradually stir in the cream. Add small quantities of the flour at a time, stirring until the flour is just incorporated after each addition. Add just enough flour to make a dough that's easy to roll out. Mix the cheese with the last of the flour you're adding. Lightly roll out the dough on a floured surface and cut into long fingers. Arrange on the greased baking sheets and bake for about 10–15 minutes or until done and golden brown. Serve as a snack.

Makes 15–18 breadsticks.

Seafood platter

Pauline prepared a selection of seafood over hot coals (the traditional West Coast way) and added a special touch by serving it topped with deep-fried rice noodles. Make up your own seafood platter with whatever is available.

Yellowtail parcels

250 ml (1 c) thinly sliced leeks
fresh fish like yellowtail, cut
  into 125 g pieces
freshly ground black pepper
salt
15 ml (1 T) olive oil
1 lemon, thinly sliced

Using 4–6 sheets of aluminium foil, make up individual fish parcels. Arrange a layer of leeks on each sheet of aluminium foil and place a piece of yellowtail on top. Sprinkle with pepper and salt and drizzle with a little of the olive oil. Top with a slice of lemon and seal the parcel around the fish. Braai the parcels over hot coals for about 6 minutes or until the fish is firm and flakes easily with a fork.

Serves 4–6 (as part of seafood platter)

breadsticks

yellowtail parcels, calamari and black mussels with deep-fried rice noodles

Braaied calamari

The secret to making melt-in-the-mouth calamari is in the cooking time: the quicker it cooks, the more tender it will be.

Slit 1 packet frozen calamari tubes on both sides to cut them in half, and remove the membrane and bony bit inside. Thaw by soaking in water to which a little milk has been added.

Heat the juice of 1 lemon, 30 ml (2 T) butter and 3 crushed garlic cloves in a pan. Arrange the calamari on the braai grid and braai over hot coals until it turns white and is no longer glassy; 3–4 minutes at the most. Baste with the lemon and garlic butter.

Serves 4–6 (as part of seafood platter).

Hint
Add a little milk to water and leave the calamari in it to soften.

Black mussels

Arrange 1 packet of frozen mussels in their half shells in a single layer on the braai grid. Blend 125 ml (½ c) mayonnaise, 125 ml (½ c) plain yoghurt, the grated rind of 1 lemon and 60 ml (4 T) chopped parsley and spoon over the mussels. Braai for about 5 minutes or until the mussels are done.

Serves 4–6 (as part of seafood platter).

Deep-fried rice noodles

Use 1 packet of Chinese rice noodles. Heat 500 ml (2 c) oil until very hot. Test by dropping a noodle strand into the oil – if it instantly curls up and turns white the oil is ready.

Place only a handful of the noodles in the hot oil at a time. Fry until they curl up and remove immediately using a slotted spoon. Sprinkle immediately with flavoured sea salt or paprika.

To serve
Place small piles of noodles on 4–6 small plates and place a piece of fish on top of each. Surround with the calamari and mussels and spoon more of the yoghurt sauce over the mussels. Garnish with sprigs of flat-leaf parsley.

baby potato and spinach salad

Lamb shanks with caramelised onions

4–6 lamb shanks (1 per person)
few sprigs fresh rosemary
100 ml olive oil
60 ml (4 T) balsamic vinegar
3 chopped shallots
salt and freshly ground black pepper to taste

Ask your butcher to saw the shanks, leaving the bones long.

Place the meat and a few sprigs of fresh rosemary in water and bring to the boil. Simmer for about 1 hour or until tender. (Do not add any salt as this will cause the meat to become tough.) Brown the shanks over the coals. Mix the remaining ingredients and use to baste the shanks while braaiing.

Serve on couscous with caramelised onions and deep-fried ginger (see recipes below).

Serves 4–6.

Caramelised onions

Stir-fry 500 g sliced onions in 60 ml (4 T) heated olive oil until glossy. Sprinkle with 60 ml (4 T) soft brown sugar and stir-fry for 1 minute. Add 50 ml balsamic vinegar and simmer until fairly sticky.

Remove from the heat and keep warm. Serve with the lamb shanks and couscous.

Makes about 500 ml.

Deep-fried ginger

Peel fresh ginger and use a vegetable peeler to slice the flesh into long strips. Fry in heated deep oil until crisp. Drain on paper towels.

Baby potato and spinach salad

canola dressing
15 ml (1 T) canola seeds
125 ml (½ c) plain yoghurt
60 ml (4 T) sunflower oil
10 ml (2 t) balsamic vinegar
brown sugar to taste
black pepper

salad
500 g baby potatoes, scrubbed
250 g baby spinach leaves
2 rounds feta cheese, broken into chunks
a few stoned black olives
a few small Rosa tomatoes
a few sprigs fresh parsley

The dressing makes this salad. It's prepared with canola seeds, now a standard crop in the Swartland (or use mustard seeds instead).

Mix all the ingredients for the dressing.

Cook the potatoes in salted water until done. Drain and cool. Combine all the salad ingredients and moisten with the dressing.

Serves 4–6.

Oven-roasted mealies and waterblommetjies

500 g waterblommetjies,
  stalks intact
2 young mealies
1 red sweet pepper, seeded
  and cut into strips
1 yellow sweet pepper,
  seeded and cut into strips
salt and freshly ground
  black pepper
juice of 1 lemon
olive oil

Rinse the waterblommetjies in salted water and remove the larger outer leaves, then cook in boiling water for 3 minutes and drain. Cook the mealies in boiling water until nearly done and cut into thick segments.

Arrange the vegetables in a single layer in an ovenproof dish and season with salt and black pepper. Add the lemon juice and drizzle with olive oil.

Bake at 200 °C (400 °F) for about 30 minutes or until the vegetables are done but still slightly crisp.

Serves 4–6.

Brandy snaps with fruit

30 ml (2 T) sugar
30 ml (2 T) butter
30 ml (2 T) golden syrup
30 ml (2 T) cake flour
7 ml (1½ t) ground ginger
10 ml (2 t) brandy

No one makes brandy snaps like Pauline's assistant, 80+-year-old Kathy Farmer.

Preheat the oven to 180 °C (350 °F) and grease a baking sheet well with butter or margarine or spray with nonstick spray and keep a muffin tin ready.

Heat the sugar, butter and golden syrup until the sugar dissolves. Let the mixture cool for 1–2 minutes. Sift the flour and ginger together, add to the butter mixture along with the brandy and mix. Drop teaspoonfuls of the mixture onto a well-greased baking sheet, leaving gaps of at least 10 cm for the snaps to spread. Bake for about 4 minutes or until golden brown and bubbles appear on the surface. Remove from the oven and leave until cool enough to handle.

Shape the brandy snaps into baskets inside the hollows of a muffin tin.

Makes about 12–15 brandy snaps.

To serve

Fill the brandy snaps with whipped cream and arrange on a bed of fresh seasonal fruit. Microwave the juice and rind of 1 lemon, a little water and 30 ml (2 T) icing sugar on 100 per cent power until the mixture just comes to the boil. Leave to cool and pour over the fruit. Garnish with a homemade chocolate finger, if desired.

brandy snaps with fruit

a gourmet braai

The fire carefully built to the cook's taste, marinated meat, braai sausage and bread toasted over the coals – for many years these have been the mainstay of any braai. Nowadays virtually anything can be prepared over the coals, from whole cuts of meat or chops to fish, side dishes and even delectable puddings. Everything is cooked to perfection – with flavours from Africa that combine happily with a touch of the Mediterranean. Even though this is an alfresco affair, the table is dressed in fine style, and paper plates and plastic glasses are banned forever.

fireside flavour

Spices add flavour to marinades and braai sauces, turning an ordinary braai into a gourmet feast. Aniseed, ginger and coriander with chicken, chillies with sweet potato – and coconut and honey turn pineapple into something special.

Vegetable flat bread with biltong

1 butternut, peeled, seeded
  and cut into pieces
1 brinjal, cut into pieces
salt
1 onion, cut into wedges
1 large red sweet pepper,
  cut into big pieces
3 baby marrows, sliced
a few broccoli florets
60 ml (4 T) olive oil
balsamic vinegar
1 kg ready-made bread dough
a few slices biltong

If you can't get bread dough, buy ready-made flat bread or pizza bases and arrange the vegetables on top.

Steam the butternut in the microwave until just done. Cool. Sprinkle the brinjal with salt and leave for 30 minutes to sweat. Rinse and pat dry. Arrange vegetables on a grid, brush with olive oil and braai over hot coals until done and slightly charred. Sprinkle with salt and a little balsamic vinegar.

Divide the dough into 6 portions, roll out into rough circles and arrange on baking sheets sprinkled with flour. Arrange roasted vegetables on each flat bread, drizzle with more olive oil and bake at 220 °C (425 °F) until done and crisp. Arrange biltong on top and return to the oven for 1 minute.

Serve with feta cheese spread (see recipe on page 24).
Serves 6.

Hint

For flat bread over the coals, place the dough on baking sheets as described and place the sheets on a griddle over very hot coals. Cook until crisp and done.

Butterflied chicken

30 ml (2 T) aniseed
10 ml (2 t) paprika
2 ml (½ t) cayenne pepper
60 ml (4 T) finely chopped
    fresh coriander
5 cm piece fresh ginger,
    grated
4 cloves garlic, crushed
juice and rind of 3 lemons
2 medium onions, finely
    chopped
250 ml (1 c) oil
salt and freshly ground
    black pepper
2 baby chickens

The unusual combination of aniseed, lemon, ginger and fresh coriander gives this dish a unique flavour.

Crush the aniseed and process with the rest of the ingredients, except the chickens, to make a marinade.

Slice through the chickens' breastbones and flatten them out. Place in a plastic bowl and pour the marinade over. Cover and marinate for 12 hours in the fridge. Bring the chickens to room temperature before braaiing them. Secure the wings and drumsticks in position with kebab skewers. Braai high over medium coals for 45–60 minutes, brushing frequently with the marinade. The chickens are done when the skin is crisp and juices run clear when a skewer is inserted into the thickest parts of the birds. Sprinkle with extra fresh coriander just before serving.

Serves 6.

Braaied sweet potatoes

6 small sweet potatoes
125 ml (½ c) olive oil
80 ml (⅓ c) lemon juice
45 ml (3 T) chopped
    fresh coriander
45 ml (3 T) honey
20 ml (4 t) freshly
    grated ginger
1 chilli, seeded and chopped
2 cloves garlic, crushed
salt and black pepper to taste

Peel sweet potatoes and slice thinly (about 3 mm thick). Place in lemon water to prevent discoloration. Cook quickly in boiling water until parcooked. Drain (ensure the slices don't break). Arrange slices in a folding braai grid and spray well with nonstick olive oil spray. Cook over hot coals until done, turning regularly. Arrange in a bowl. Mix the olive oil with the rest of the ingredients. Pour over the hot sweet potatoes.

Serve hot or cold.

Serves 6.

butterflied chicken

braaied pineapple with coconut cream

Cucumber and feta salad

2 English cucumbers,
  thickly sliced
250 g feta cheese, cubed
60 ml (4 T) olive oil
30 ml (2 T) lemon juice
8 spring onions, chopped
60 ml (4 T) chopped
  fresh fennel
60 ml (4 T) chopped
  fresh mint
salt and freshly ground black
  pepper to taste

Fresh mint and fennel flavour this fresh salad.

Sprinkle the cucumber with salt and allow to stand for 30 minutes. Squeeze dry. Place in a salad bowl. Add the feta cheese. Mix the rest of the ingredients and pour over. Chill until needed.
  Serves 4–6.

Yoghurt and spanspek salad

1 spanspek or pawpaw,
  peeled and cubed
2 mangoes or bananas, sliced
250 ml (1 c) plain yoghurt
5 ml (1 t) honey
15 ml (1 T) chopped
  fresh mint
salt and freshly ground
  black pepper to taste
60 ml (4 T) toasted
  sesame seeds

Sprinkle a fresh fruit salad with toasted sesame seeds for a crunchy texture.

Mix the fruit in a bowl. Make a dressing from the yoghurt, honey, mint and salt and pepper to taste. Pour over the salad and sprinkle with the toasted sesame seeds.
  Serves 4–6.

Braaied pineapple with coconut cream

250 ml (1 c) cream
80 ml (⅓ c) toasted coconut
2 large pineapples, quartered
  (with stalk intact)
honey
60 ml (4 T) chopped
  cashew nuts

Yum!

Mix the cream and toasted coconut well and set aside. Braai the pineapples lightly over the coals until browned here and there. Cut the flesh from the skin and cut into chunks. Drizzle with honey. Sprinkle with the chopped nuts and serve with coconut cream. Serve lukewarm.
  Serves 6.

Variation
Cube the pineapple flesh and place in a bowl. Sprinkle with coconut and nuts and serve with fresh cream sweetened with honey.

budget braai

Pilchards, ribs or Texan steak are all affordable braai choices. Pep up bread dough with herbs and make vegetable kebabs, sambals and salads, which are just as economical.

Grilled pilchards or harders

1 kg pilchards or harders,
  heads intact (gut them only
  if bigger than 12 cm)
3 cloves garlic, crushed
juice and rind of 1 lemon
15 ml (1 T) finely chopped
  fresh parsley
15 ml (1 T) finely chopped
  fresh coriander
large pinch each curry
  powder, cumin and turmeric
salt and freshly ground black
  pepper to taste
lemon wedges

Pilchards take only a few minutes to cook over the fire. Serve them as a starter while you braai the meat.

Place the pilchards in a flat glass dish. Mix the remaining ingredients except the lemon wedges and pour over. Leave for an hour. Drain and braai over hot coals, about 5–10 minutes a side until just cooked through. (If using a closed braai, e.g. a Weber, it is unnecessary to turn the pilchards.)
  Serve with the lemon wedges.
  Serves 6.

Caribbean pork spareribs

1 kg pork ribs
lemon wedges

Caribbean marinade
1 onion, finely chopped
juice and rind of 1 lemon
90 ml (6 T) olive oil
1 chilli, seeded and chopped
10 ml (2 t) allspice
5 cloves garlic, crushed
2 ml (½ t) dried thyme
2 ml (½ t) dried chilli flakes
2 ml (½ t) grated nutmeg
5 ml (1 t) grated fresh ginger
salt and freshly ground
  black pepper
60 ml (4 T) rum (optional)
45 ml (3 T) soft brown sugar
10–15 bay leaves

Spareribs are a treat. Instead of pork spareribs you can use a rack of lamb.

Place the ribs in a shallow dish. Mix all the ingredients for the marinade and pour over the ribs. Leave to marinate overnight. Drain and braai the ribs for about 35–45 minutes or until cooked through and crisp on the outside. Brush frequently with extra marinade.
  Serve with the lemon wedges.
  Serves 6.

Texan steak

1 Texan steak (about 2–4 kg),
  seasoned with braai spices
  or coated with marinade
  and vacuum-packed

This is butcher Alan Allsop's name for this huge steak cut from a round of beef. It's one of the most affordable whole beef cuts available. Ask for meat that comes from a young animal and has been well-matured.

Place the meat high above hot coals moved slightly to the edge of the braai area. Braai for about 40 minutes or until the meat is brown on the outside but still slightly pink inside.
  Serve with Creole rémoulade (see recipe below).
  Serves 6.

Creole rémoulade

Finely chop 2 spring onions and mix with 60–80 ml (4–5 T) mayonnaise, 1 finely chopped clove garlic, 30–45 ml (2–3 T) whole-grain mustard, 5 ml (1 t) crushed capers, 2 ml (½ t) paprika, black pepper to taste, 10 ml (2 t) olive oil and the juice of ¼ lemon.
  Serve with the steak.
  Makes about 125 ml (½ c).

Braai sauce

2 onions, chopped
250 ml (1 c) tomato sauce
180 ml (¾ c) light
  brown sugar
2 cloves garlic, crushed
5 ml (1 t) mustard powder
5 ml (1 t) ground ginger
5 ml (1 t) cayenne pepper
salt and pepper

A delicious sauce for brushing over meat being braaied. This one is also excellent with braaied brown mushrooms.

Place all the ingredients in a pan over medium heat. Stir occasionally until the sugar has dissolved. Bring to the boil and simmer for 30–40 minutes or until fragrant. Cool and use as required. The sauce will keep in the fridge for a week.
   Makes 500 ml (2 c).

Variation
Prepare a rub using 25 g cumin seeds, 25 g coriander seeds, 6 ml chilli flakes, 6 ml whole peppercorns and coarse salt. Grind the mixture finely and rub into the meat instead of the braai spices or braai sauce. Leave for 30 minutes.

Vegetable and cheese kebabs

3–4 large long-life tomatoes,
  cut into 8 wedges
250 g mozzarella cheese,
  cubed
spinach leaves or fresh
  bay leaves
3 cloves garlic, crushed
dried chilli flakes
60 ml (4 T) olive oil

Thread tomatoes, cheese and spinach onto skewers for these quick kebabs.

Place the tomatoes, cheese and spinach or bay leaves in a dish. Mix the garlic and chilli flakes with the olive oil and sprinkle on top. Leave for at least 15 minutes. Thread the ingredients onto skewers, alternating them, and braai over hot coals for about 3 minutes or until the cheese has melted. Serve immediately with the herb loaf and extra garlic oil.
   Serves 4–6.

Herb spiral loaf

Mix 250 ml (1 c) freshly chopped mixed herbs with 125 ml (½ c) olive oil. Roll out 1 kg prepared bread dough, spread the herb mixture on top and roll into a spiral. Place on a greased baking sheet. Leave to rise in a warm place until double in volume.
   In the meantime, preheat the oven to190 °C (375 °F).
   Bake the bread for about 40 minutes until done. Serve luke-warm with butter.
   Makes 1 large or 2 medium loaves.

vegetable and cheese kebabs

Sambal and salad selection

Serve an array of sambals and salad in mugs or bowls.

Wheat salad

1 packet (100 g) almond
  flakes
60 g butter
2 onions, thinly sliced
2 ml (½ t) ground cinnamon
1 ml (¼ t) ground cumin
250 g pearl wheat
500 ml (2 c) chicken stock
100 g raisins

dressing
75 ml (5 T) sunflower oil
juice and rind of 1 orange
1–2 garlic cloves
15–30 ml (1–2 T) honey
15 ml (1 T) whole-grain or
  Dijon mustard
fresh coriander or mint

Stir-fry the almond flakes in a dry pan until golden brown. Remove from the pan. Melt the butter and stir-fry the onions with the spices until tender.

Cook the pearl wheat in chicken stock until tender, adding the raisins about 5 minutes before the end of the cooking time so they can plump up. Drain and mix with the almonds and onion mixture.

Mix all the ingredients for the dressing and pour over the wheat mixture while still hot. Cool and store in the fridge until needed. Garnish with fresh herbs.

Serves 6.

sambal and salad selection

Cabbage sambal

¼ cabbage, shredded
2 onions, chopped
chopped mint or
    coriander leaves
30 ml (2 T) oil
juice of 1 lemon
salt and pepper

Combine the cabbage, onions and herbs. Blend the oil and lemon juice and pour over. Season with salt and pepper.
    Serves 4–6.

Tangy onion rings

3 onions, sliced into rings
60 ml (4 T) olive oil
6 bay leaves
2 ml (½ t) oregano
pinch ground allspice
125 ml (½ c) grape vinegar
1 garlic clove, crushed
15 ml (1 T) soft brown sugar
large pinch ground cumin
salt

Separate the onion rings and mix with the remaining ingredients. Leave in the fridge overnight before spooning into a sterilised jar and sealing. The onion rings will keep for a year.
    Makes about 500 ml (2 c).

Tomato salsa

3–5 garlic cloves, crushed
1 small onion, chopped
15 ml (1 T) finely chopped
    fresh parsley
15 ml (1 T) finely chopped
    fresh coriander
5-7 ripe tomatoes, chopped
15 ml (1 T) lemon juice
olive oil
salt and pepper to taste
1–2 red chillies, seeded
    and chopped

Combine all the ingredients and spoon into small bowls.
    Makes about 500 ml (2 c).

Watermelon platter

¼ watermelon
small spanspek
strawberries and/or
    other berries
oranges, nectarines and/or
    bananas, cut into pieces
45 ml (3 T) orange juice
2 pieces ginger preserve,
    finely chopped
45 ml (3 T) ginger syrup

A refreshing summertime dessert. The ginger and orange syrup enhances the flavour of the fruit.

Cut the fruit into pieces and arrange on a large platter. Mix the orange juice with the ginger preserve and syrup and pour over the fruit. Serve with plain yoghurt sweetened with a little honey. Garnish with fresh mint.

hot off the coals

Contemporary flavours add an exciting twist to traditional braai meats and salads.

Beef fillet with
  mussel sauce
Chicken with white
  wine sauce
Barracuda
Roast vegetables with
  savoury couscous
Bacon and vegetables with
  mustard sauce

Avocado salad with
  oriental dressing
Piquant couscous salad
Brown rice salad with nuts
  and sun-dried tomatoes
Potato salad with olives,
  gherkins and egg
Pear and poppy seed salad
Lentil and raisin salad

Beef fillet with mussel sauce

marrow bones, 5 cm thick
1 beef fillet
freshly ground salt and
  black pepper
250 ml (1 c) grated pecorino
  or Parmesan cheese

mussel sauce
250 ml (1 c) cream
1 can (185 g) smoked
  mussels, drained
about 10 ml (2 t) instant white
  sauce powder

This is how the West Coast Winelands team shows its mettle when competing in the braai championships.

Heat marrow bones until the marrow is cooked. Chill. Using a sharp knife, make shallow incisions all over the fillet and stuff with the marrow. Season with salt and pepper and braai rapidly over hot coals until brown on the outside but still pink inside – about 15 minutes. Press the cheese on top of the fillet and cover with aluminium foil so the cheese will melt. Keep warm while preparing the mussel sauce.

Bring the cream and mussels to the boil. Blend the white sauce powder with a little water and stir into the cream mixture. Bring to the boil and simmer until the sauce thickens.

To serve: Carefully cut the fillet into fairly thick slices and pour the sauce over.

Serves 4.

beef fillet with mussel sauce

Roast vegetables with savoury couscous

roast vegetables
6 baby marrows, sliced
1 red sweet pepper, seeded
  and cut into strips
1 yellow sweet pepper,
  seeded and cut into strips
125 g fresh young asparagus
6 brown mushrooms, sliced
a few cherry tomatoes
bunch of spring onions
olive oil

couscous
250 ml (1 c) couscous
250 ml (1 c) boiling water
30 ml (2 T) olive oil
3 sun-dried tomatoes,
  finely chopped
80 ml (⅓ c) readymade
  vinaigrette
15–30 ml (1–2 T) readymade
  basil pesto

Adelé Wessels, well-known caterer from Heidelberg, Cape, serves these vegetables as a starter or a side dish at a braai.

Preheat the oven to 200 °C (400 °F). Place all the vegetables, except the spring onions, in a single layer in an ovenproof dish. Drizzle with olive oil and roast for about 20 minutes or until just tender but still firm to the bite. Slice the spring onions diagonally into long pieces, heat enough olive oil in a saucepan and deep-fry the spring onions until crisp. Set aside.

Prepare the couscous with boiling water according to the packet instructions. Stir in the olive oil, sun-dried tomatoes, vinaigrette and pesto. Add the roast vegetables and mix lightly. Scatter the spring onions on top and serve.

Serves 4–6.

roast vegetables with savoury couscous

Barracuda

2–3 kg barracuda or
 yellowtail, head and tail
 removed
salt to taste
10 ml (2 t) fish spice
6 garlic cloves, crushed
200 g butter
7 ml (1½ t) dried oregano
juice of 2 lemons

marinade
250 ml (1 c) oil
125 ml (½ c) olive oil
75 ml (5 T) Spillers peri-
 peri oil
375 ml (1½ c) dry white wine
juice of 1 large lemon
3 sprigs fresh rosemary
1 bunch chives, chopped
freshly ground black pepper

At fish braais on the north coast of Natal barracuda is the fish of choice. As it is inclined to be on the dry side, it is braaied slowly in a flavoursome garlic sauce that soaks into the flesh, making it deliciously juicy. This fish is best steam-braaied slowly in a covered gas or Weber braai.

Wash the fish well and pat dry. Place it in an oven dish and make deep slashes in the flesh, about 5 cm apart. Rub in the salt and fish spice. Mix the garlic, butter and oregano, and rub into the slashes. Spread the remaining butter mixture on top and along the sides of the fish. Sprinkle the lemon juice over the fish.

To make the marinade blend the oil, olive oil, peri-peri oil, white wine and lemon juice and pour over the fish. Place the rosemary sprigs and chives alongside the fish. Season the fish with a little freshly ground black pepper and leave it to marinate in the refrigerator for about 24 hours.

Cook the fish in a covered gas or Weber braai or in the oven at 150 °C (300 °F) for about 1½–2 hours. Place the cooked fish on a serving platter, pour over the remaining marinade and serve with plenty of lemon wedges and savoury rice, Italian bread and a salad made with mango, pineapple and litchi.

Serves 6–8.

Cook's notes

- Instead of barracuda you can use any firm fish such as yellowtail. The cooking time will depend on the thickness of the fish.
- The secret is to allow the fish to cook slowly as it's fairly thick. Reduce the cooking time for a thinner fish. The fish is cooked when the flesh flakes easily with a fork.
- Cover the fish with aluminium foil if baking in the oven.
- The hottest part of a chilli is the seeds – remove them if you prefer your food less fiery. Green chillies also tend to be hotter than red ones.

chicken with white wine sauce and charred waterblommetjie

Chicken with white wine sauce

8 chicken pieces
salt and freshly ground
   black pepper
whole-grain mustard
50 ml olive oil

Season the chicken with salt and pepper and spread with whole-grain mustard and oil. Braai slowly over medium coals for about half an hour or until cooked and golden brown on the outside. Turn frequently. Serve with steamed waterblommetjies, charred over the coals, and white wine sauce.
   Serves 6–8.

White wine sauce

200 ml white wine
1 egg
30 ml (2 T) sugar
30 ml (2 T) whole-grain
   mustard
30 ml (2 T) lemon juice

Mix all the ingredients for the sauce in a heat-resistant glass bowl. Place over a saucepan of boiling water and heat, stirring continuously, until the sauce thickens and is cooked through. Alternatively, microwave until done.
   Makes about 200 ml.

Bacon and vegetables with mustard sauce

sauce
125 ml (½ c) sugar or honey
12 ml (2½ t) mustard powder
7 ml (1½ t) cake flour
salt to taste
60 ml (4 T) grape vinegar
1 extra-large egg, whisked
100 ml plain yoghurt

vegetables
125 g bacon, shredded
350 g baby marrows, sliced
250 g mushrooms, sliced
500 ml (2 c) croutons

A favourite dish from Adelé Wessels, Heidelberg (Cape) and a hit at any braai.

Blend together all the ingredients for the sauce except the egg and yoghurt. Heat slowly on the stove top (stirring continuously) or in the microwave oven (stirring occasionally) until the sauce just comes to the boil and thickens. Remove from the heat, mix a little of the sauce with the whisked egg and return everything to the remaining sauce. Heat slowly until the sauce just comes to the boil. Cool and stir in the yoghurt. Store in the fridge.
   Fry the bacon until golden brown and crisp. Remove from the pan and set aside. Stir-fry the baby marrows and mushrooms in the bacon fat until tender but still firm to the bite. Mix with the salad sauce and bacon. Add the croutons just before serving.
   Serves 4–6.

Avocado salad with oriental dressing

2 avocados, peeled and
  sliced into wedges
lemon juice
300 g red lettuce leaves,
  torn into pieces
2 large red onions,
  thinly sliced
200 g Portabellini
  mushrooms, thinly sliced

dressing
60 ml (4 T) olive oil
juice of 1 lime
30 ml (2 T) honey
2,5 cm piece fresh ginger,
  peeled and finely grated
30 ml (2 T) mustard seeds
salt and freshly ground
  black pepper

Leave the salad for an hour or two to allow the flavours to develop and serve at room temperature. The honey and ginger in the dressing complement the avocado perfectly. For a starter, use fewer lettuce leaves and arrange the salad on individual plates.

Sprinkle the avocado wedges with lemon juice and mix with the lettuce leaves, onions and mushrooms. Beat together the ingredients for the dressing and pour over the salad.
  Serves 6–8.

Piquant couscous salad

375 ml (1½ c) couscous
250 ml (1 c) boiling water
125 ml (½ c) white wine
salt and freshly ground
  black pepper
2 red sweet peppers, seeded
  and finely chopped
2 red onions, finely chopped
20 g flat-leaf parsley,
  finely chopped
25 ml (5 t) fresh mint,
  finely chopped
60 ml (4 T) olive oil
juice of 1 large lemon

Couscous salad is always a hit. It's quick and easy to make and tastes even better if made a day in advance and left in the fridge.

Place the couscous in n large bowl. Bring the water and white wine to the boil and pour over the couscous. Leave until all the liquid has been absorbed. Fluff with a fork, then microwave for 2 minutes. Fluff once more with a fork to separate the grains. Season with salt and pepper and add the vegetables and herbs. Beat the olive oil and lemon juice together and pour over the salad. Mix and leave to stand for about 1 hour to allow the flavours to develop.
Serves 6–8.

Brown rice salad with nuts and sun-dried tomatoes

500 ml (2 c) uncooked
  brown rice
90 ml (6 T) olive oil
30 ml (2 T) red wine vinegar
salt and freshly ground
  black pepper
200 g mixed nuts,
  coarsely chopped
200 g sun-dried tomatoes in
  vinaigrette, chopped

This fibre-rich nutty salad is a great buffet dish and goes well with cold meats.

Cook the rice until done, drain and set aside. Make a dressing by mixing the oil and vinegar and seasoning with salt and freshly ground black pepper. Lightly mix the rice with the nuts and sun-dried tomatoes and moisten with the dressing. Serve as a side dish.
  Serves 6–8.

Potato salad with olives, gherkins and egg

1 kg baby potatoes, scrubbed
  and halved
30 ml (2 T) olive oil
salt and freshly ground black
  pepper to taste
6 chives, chopped
150 ml gherkins, chopped
75 g olives
1-2 hard-boiled eggs

salad dressing
45 ml (3 T) olive oil
15 ml (1 T) white wine vinegar
5 ml (1 t) whole-grain mustard
salt and freshly ground black
  pepper to taste

A lighter version of conventional potato salad.

Boil the potatoes until done. Meanwhile, make the dressing by beating together all the ingredients. Season with salt and freshly ground black pepper.

Drain the potatoes once soft, add the 30 ml (2 T) olive oil and season with salt and pepper. Break the potatoes into pieces with a fork. Add the chives, gherkins and olives and mix. Shell the eggs, chop coarsely and add to the salad. Moisten the salad with the dressing and mix lightly.

Serves 6.

Pear and poppy seed salad

300 g baby spinach and
  watercress
200 g Portabellini mushrooms
5 pears, rinsed, cored and
  sliced into wedges
1 red onion, thinly sliced

salad dressing
45 ml (3 T) olive oil
15 ml (1 T) white wine vinegar
5 ml (1 t) whole-grain mustard
15 ml (1 T) poppy seeds

The textures and flavours in this salad combine beautifully. You can use butter lettuce instead of the spinach and apples instead of pears.

Combine the spinach, watercress, mushrooms, pears and onion. Make a dressing by beating together the oil, vinegar and mustard and moisten the salad with the dressing. Sprinkle the poppy seeds on top.

Serves 6–8.

Lentil and raisin salad

150 g seedless raisins
juice and finely grated rind
  of 2 small oranges
625 ml (2½ c) cooked
  brown lentils
large bunch of flat-leaf
  parsley, finely chopped
salt and freshly ground
  black pepper
60 ml (4 T) olive oil
15 ml (1 T) white wine vinegar
2 ml (½ t) ground cumin
2 ml (½ t) mustard seeds
5 ml (1 t) roasted curry
  powder

Lentils and raisins go well together. Serve this salad with bread and cold meats or as part of a vegetarian meal.

Soak the raisins in the orange juice overnight. Add the rind, lentils and parsley. Season with salt and pepper. Mix the olive oil, vinegar, cumin, mustard seeds and curry powder together until well blended and pour over the lentil mixture. Adjust the seasoning and leave the salad to stand for 1 hour before serving.

Serves 6–8.

perfect picnic

Water ripples over river pebbles, and every now and again red-knobbed coots and ducks come looking for scraps of food. Fishing lines have been cast – even though it won't really matter if the fish don't bite today. The river boat glides slowly through the water, followed by boisterous children in rubber tubes; the sound of cheerful voices from the boat competes with the raucous cries of finches in the reeds.

gone fishing

Spend a day at the riverside and tuck into delicious home-made treats from the picnic basket.

picnic loaf

Mustard straws

oil for spreading
550 ml (2¼ c) cake flour
10 ml (2 t) mustard powder
5 ml (1 t) salt
10 ml (2 t) baking powder
3 ml (generous ½ t) paprika
  or cayenne pepper
250 g cold butter
10 ml (2 t) whole-grain
  mustard
310 ml (1¼ c) grated
  Cheddar cheese
30-40 ml ice-cold water
1 extra-large egg, beaten

Ideal to nibble on while you wait for the big one to bite. This recipe is an interesting variation on traditional cheese straws.

Preheat the oven to 230 °C (450 °F) and grease a baking sheet with olive oil or spray with nonstick spray.

Mix the dry ingredients. Grate the butter and rub gently into the flour with your fingertips until the mixture resembles fine breadcrumbs. Add the mustard, cheese and enough ice-cold water to form a stiff dough. Roll the dough out to 6 mm thickness and brush with the beaten egg. Cut into strips, giving each strip a couple of twists, and bake for 10 minutes or until golden brown and done. Cool on the baking sheet for a few minutes, then transfer to a wire rack to cool completely. Store in an airtight container.

Makes about 15.

Picnic loaf

100 g each black and green
  olives, stoned and chopped
60 ml (4 T) olive oil
60 ml (4 T) chopped parsley
1 red sweet red pepper and
1 green sweet pepper,
  seeded, roasted
  and skinned
5 ml (1 t) chopped fresh
  oregano
juice of 1 small lemon
salt and freshly ground
  black pepper
1 large Italian loaf, such
  as ciabatta
a few lettuce leaves
8–10 slices salami
100 g Cheddar cheese,
  thinly sliced

Hollow out a large Italian loaf and stuff with salami, sweet peppers and olives.

Mix the olives, oil, parsley, sweet peppers, oregano, lemon juice, salt and black pepper and chill overnight. Slice open the loaf and remove some of the soft dough to make room for the stuffing. Drain the olive mixture and spread the inside of the loaf with the marinade. Spoon half the olive mixture into the loaf and top with the lettuce, salami and cheese. Spoon over the rest of the olive mixture and top with the upper half of the loaf. Wrap tightly in cling film and leave in the fridge for at least 30 minutes with a heavy weight on top. Remove and leave out until it reaches room temperature. Cut into slices.
  Serves 4–6.

Spiced nuts

Sauté 500 ml (2 c) mixed nuts in 25 ml (5 t) butter over low heat. Mix 50 ml (10 t) sugar, 3 ml (generous ½ t) paprika, 3 ml (generous ½ t) ground cumin, 2 ml (½ t) ground coriander, 1 ml (¼ t) chilli powder, 2 ml (½ t) black pepper and 3 ml (generous ½ t) salt and sprinkle over the nuts. Stir-fry until golden. Spoon onto a sheet of aluminium foil and cool. Store in an airtight container.
  Makes 500 ml (2 c) nuts.

mustard straws

phyllo cheese tartlets

Phyllo cheese tartlets

olive oil
8–10 sheets phyllo pastry
150 g feta cheese
150 g ricotta cheese
100 g mozzarella cheese,
  grated
60 ml (4 T) sour cream
3–4 piquanté peppers,
  finely chopped
salt and freshly ground
  black pepper

*Three cheeses, baked in phyllo pastry – and so easy to prepare.
Enjoy with a sweet chilli sauce.*

Preheat the oven to 180 °C (350 °F) and lightly grease 3 tart
tins, 15 cm in diameter, with olive oil. Line with phyllo pastry,
brushing each piece of pastry with olive oil. Mix the feta,
ricotta, mozzarella, sour cream and piquanté peppers and
season with salt and pepper. Spoon the cheese mixture into
the tart tins, fold over the phyllo and seal. Bake for 25 minutes
until golden brown.
  Serve lukewarm with a sweet chilli sauce.
  Makes 3 small tarts.

Fillet salad with roasted vegetables

meat
1 beef fillet (about 300 g)
olive oil
salt and freshly ground
  black pepper
Dijon mustard

salad
olive oil
1 large onion, sliced into very
  thin wedges
4 garlic cloves, chopped
1 red sweet pepper, seeded
  and sliced into strips
1 green sweet pepper, seeded
  and sliced into strips
1 container (250 g) cherry
  tomatoes
4 baby marrows, sliced
salt and pepper

herb vinaigrette
60 ml (4 T) olive oil
30 ml (2 T) lemon juice or
  balsamic vinegar
45 ml (3 T) chopped fresh
  herbs like parsley, oregano,
  rosemary
2 garlic cloves, crushed

*Make the salad a day earlier to allow flavours to blend. A brilliant
idea to make use of leftover fillet.*

Brush the fillet with olive oil, season with salt and pepper and
spread lightly with mustard. Stand for about 30 minutes.
  Meanwhile, turn the oven grill on high. When hot, grill the
fillet for 5 minutes on each side (depending on thickness) until browned and done on the outside but still pink inside. Let
the meat rest for a few minutes.
  Pour a little olive oil into an oven pan and roast the vegetables until done and the edges begin to char. Slice the meat
very thinly and mix with the vegetables. Mix all the ingredients for the herb vinaigrette and moisten the salad. Season
to taste with salt and pepper.
  Serves 6.

Chickpea purée with pitta triangles

2 cans (400 g each)
  chickpeas, drained
5 ml (1 t) salt
45 ml (3 T) lemon juice
3 garlic cloves, crushed
80 ml (⅓ c) olive oil

Process the chickpeas, salt, lemon juice, garlic and olive oil until smooth. Adapt seasoning to taste and chill until needed. Serve with pitta triangles (see below) or bread.

  Makes 500 ml (2 c) purée.

Hint
The purée will dry out a little if left to stand. To moisten, add a little olive oil and mix well.

Pitta triangles

Halve a few pittas and cut into triangles. Brush lightly with olive oil and sprinkle with sesame seeds. Preheat the oven to 180 °C (350 °F). Arrange pittas in a single layer on a baking sheet and bake until golden brown and crisp. Allow to cool and store in an airtight container.

Date and chocolate cake

250 g soft butter
180 ml (¾ c) castor sugar
2 extra-large eggs
250 g dates, finely chopped
125 ml (½ c) desiccated
  coconut
125 ml (½ c) cooked and
  mashed pumpkin
15 ml (1 T) finely grated
  orange rind
450 ml self-raising flour
50 ml cocoa powder
pinch of salt
125 ml (½ c) milk

Preheat the oven to 160 °C (325 °F) and grease a 24 cm diameter cake tin with butter or margarine or spray with non-stick spray. Line tin with baking paper.

  Cream the butter and sugar until light and creamy. Beat in the eggs one at a time, beating well after each addition. Stir in the dates, coconut, pumpkin and orange rind.

  Sift the self-raising flour, cocoa powder and salt together and stir into the butter mixture, alternating with the milk.

  Spoon the batter into the tin and bake for 1½ hours until done or a skewer inserted into the cake comes out clean. Allow to cool for 10 minutes in the tin. Turn out onto a wire rack and cool completely. Cut into squares and sift icing sugar and cocoa alternately over the squares.

  Makes 1 medium cake.

river cruise

The African Queen offers regular cruises on the Klein River which flows past Stanford, on beyond Hermanus. On this river boat Marlene Swart's delectable food puts everyone in a cheerful, social mood.

Deep-fried calamari and perlemoen

Thaw frozen calamari rings. Clean the perlemoen, beat lightly with a wooden mallet and prick with a fork. Cut into strips. Dip the calamari rings and perlemoen strips into beaten egg, then in cake flour and deep-fry for not more than 1 minute until golden brown.

Serve immediately with lemon wedges.

Fish platter

lettuce leaves
cucumber slices
smooth cottage cheese
strips of smoked salmon
dill sprigs
whole-wheat bread, brushed
  with olive oil and toasted
pepper mackerel, flaked into
  bite-size pieces
sour fig jam
lemon slices

Cover a platter with a selection of lettuce leaves. Spread a few cucumber slices with smooth cottage cheese and top with a piece of salmon and fresh dill sprigs. Slice the toast into fingers and arrange on the platter along with the mackerel. Top with small scoops of jam if desired.

Garnish with lemon slices.

Iron-pot leg of lamb

1,5 kg leg of lamb
salt and freshly ground
  black pepper
mustard powder
crushed garlic
Worcester sauce
1 onion, coarsely chopped
olive oil

Marlene cooks the leg in a cast-iron pot in the oven. You can even cook it over the coals.

Preheat the oven to 180 °C (350 °F) and grease a fairly large cast-iron pot with oil.

Place the leg of lamb on a work surface. Mix the salt, pepper, mustard powder, garlic and Worcester sauce to taste and spread over the surface of the leg. Fry the onion in a little olive oil until tender. Spread over the base of the pot and place the leg of lamb on top. Cover and bake for about 2½ hours or until tender and done.

Slice and serve at room temperature with mint sauce to which you've added a little chopped onion, green sweet pepper and a curry mayonnaise sauce (see chicken kebabs recipe on page 80). Serve with oven-roasted vegetables and stuffed prunes (see recipe below).

Serves 6.

Stuffed prunes

125 ml (½ c) dried apricots,
  finely chopped
½ onion, very finely chopped
15 ml (1 T) parsley,
  finely chopped
1 chilli, seeded and finely
  chopped
250 g prunes, stoned

Marlene Swart makes a stuffing of stewed dried apricots, flavoured with chilli.

Slowly stew the apricots in a little water until tender. Chop finely and mix with the onion, parsley and chilli. Stuff the prunes with the mixture and serve with the leg of lamb.

Hint
Wrap a prune in a slice of roast lamb and secure by tying with chives.

fish platter

Chicken kebabs

2 chicken breasts, skinned
  and boned
freshly ground black pepper
  to taste
3 ml (generous ½ t) Aromat
25 ml (5 t) lemon juice
1 chicken stock cube
15 dried apricots
4 kebab skewers

sauce
125 ml (½ c) thick plain
  yoghurt
125 ml (½ c) thick
  mayonnaise
2 ml (½ t) curry powder
1 ml (¼ t) cumin (jeera)

Preheat the oven to 180 °C (350 °F) and lightly oil a small ovenproof dish. Season the chicken breasts with salt, pepper, Aromat and lemon juice. Dissolve the chicken stock cube in a little water, add, cover and bake for 30 minutes. Leave to cool and cut into bite-size pieces. Thread chicken pieces onto kebab skewers, alternating with apricots.

Mix the yoghurt, mayonnaise and spices and pour over the chicken. Leave to stand for a while before serving.

Makes 4 small kebabs.

Oven-roasted vegetables

olive oil
a selection of vegetables
  such as green beans,
  carrots, whole garlic,
  sweet potatoes, baby gem
  squashes or marrows,
  broccoli, cauliflower, variety
  of sweet peppers
salt and freshly ground black
  pepper to taste
lemon juice
fresh herbs such as rosemary,
  parsley, sage and thyme

Preheat the oven to 200 °C (400 °F) and pour a little olive oil in a large ovenproof dish.

Rinse the vegetables and pat dry. Peel the vegetables as needed and cut everything into fairly large chunks. Arrange the hardest vegetables in the ovenproof dish. Season with salt and pepper and roast for 10 minutes, then start adding the other vegetables. Add the soft vegetables last. Oven-roast until everything is done, but still crisp. Season once more with salt and pepper, lemon juice and fresh herbs and serve hot or at room temperature.

Cheese and onion bread

500 g self-raising flour
1 packet (65 g) thick white
  onion soup powder
1 ml (¼ t) salt
5 ml (1 t) baking powder
150 g Cheddar cheese, grated
1 extra-large egg
500 ml (2 c) buttermilk

Preheat the oven to 180 °C (350 °F) and grease a 1,5 litre loaf tin with butter or margarine or spray with nonstick spray.

Sift the flour, onion soup powder, salt and baking powder together. Add 100 g of the cheese and mix well. Beat the egg and buttermilk together and add to the dry ingredients. Stir well. Turn the batter into the prepared tin, spreading evenly.

Sprinkle the remaining cheese on top and bake for 1 hour until done or a skewer inserted into the centre of the bread comes out clean.

Serve with a selection of cheeses and jam.

Makes 1 medium loaf.

Chocolate crispies

175 g butter
175 g (1¾ slabs) milk
  chocolate, broken into
  pieces
180 ml (¾ c) golden syrup
175 g Rice Krispies

Delicious with coffee.

Melt the butter, chocolate and golden syrup in the microwave oven on 75 per cent power, stirring occasionally until smooth. Pour the chocolate sauce over the Rice Krispies and mix. Spoon mounds of the mixture into paper cases and leave for 8 hours to set.
  Makes about 25.

cheese and onion bread

the magic of
the veld

The veld has a unique charm. Here children can play undisturbed and grown-ups laugh and relax in the fresh air. In spring we are treated to a spectacular display of flowers and tender new grass, and at dusk the last rays of the sun paint the sky in shades of pink, spelling romance. Time to put out the chairs and enjoy what the picnic basket has to offer.

romantic picnic

Surprise your loved one with a picnic in the veld. Devise a menu in shades of red and pack everything in tins decorated with red raffia and hearts fashioned from wire.

Menu
Sparkling wine

Ice-cold strawberry and
   yoghurt soup
Green salad with mint
   vinaigrette
Red pepper pâté with
   heart-shaped crisp bread
Spinach and goat's milk
   cheese roulade

Petits fours
Iced coffee with
   shortbread hearts

Ice-cold strawberry and yoghurt soup

300 g strawberries, hulled,
   washed and halved
125 ml (½ c) rosé wine
125 ml (½ c) plain yoghurt
60 ml (4 T) milk or cream
black pepper and a pinch
   of sugar

A recipe received from Laetitia Prinsloo of The Institute of Culinary Arts in Stellenbosch.

Marinate the strawberries overnight in the wine. Pour into a saucepan and simmer for 20 minutes or until the strawberries are just tender. Cool to room temperature and chill until ice cold. Pureé until smooth. Add the yoghurt and milk or cream and season to taste with black pepper and sugar. Serve cold with extra ice cubes and berries.

   For the picnic: Pour the chilled soup into a vacuum flask. Makes about 1 litre.

Hint
If fresh strawberries aren't obtainable use 325 ml fresh strawberry juice.

Green salad with mint vinaigrette

salad
150 g mangetout
200 g mixed lettuce leaves
60 g red cabbage, shredded
salt and freshly ground
  black pepper

dressing
juice and finely grated rind
  of 1 lemon
30 ml (2 T) olive oil
15 ml (1 T) finely chopped
  fresh mint
10 ml (2 t) runny honey

Blanch the mangetout by plunging them into boiling water for 1 minute, then rinsing under cold water until completely cold. Pat dry and cut into long, fairly thick strips. Tear the lettuce leaves into smaller pieces.

Gently mix the mangetout strips and lettuce with the remaining ingredients. Whisk together all the ingredients for the dressing and chill.

Drizzle over the salad just before serving.

Serves 4–6.

Red pepper pâté with heart-shaped crisp bread

500 g red sweet peppers
500 g red plum tomatoes
30 ml (2 T) olive oil
3 garlic cloves, unpeeled
handful of fresh basil
5 ml (1 t) coarse salt
45 ml (3 T) lemon juice
freshly ground black pepper

This flavoursome pâté keeps well in the fridge. Use any leftover pâté in savoury tarts or for flavouring frittatas.

Preheat the oven to 180 °C (350 °F) and keep a baking sheet at hand. Halve and seed the sweet peppers and tomatoes, and arrange them on the baking sheet. Drizzle with 15 ml (1 T) olive oil and roast for 1 hour, turning occasionally. Add the garlic and roast for another 30 minutes or until the garlic is soft and the skin of the peppers is charred. Leave the vegetables to cool before removing the skins. Process the sweet peppers and tomatoes in a food processor along with the remaining ingredients until smooth. Spoon into a dish and chill the pâté for at least 4 hours before serving to allow the flavours to develop. Serve with heart-shaped crisp bread.

Makes about 800 ml.

To make the heart-shaped crisp bread
Thinly slice a white loaf and cut out heart shapes with a cookie cutter. Dry the slices in the oven at 100 °C (200 °F). Store in an airtight container.

Spinach and goat's milk cheese roulade

250 g cooked spinach
50 ml cake flour
2 ml (½ t) grated nutmeg
30 ml (2 T) chopped
  fresh chives
salt and freshly ground black
  pepper to taste
3 extra-large eggs, separated

filling
100 g soft goat's milk cheese
200 g cream cheese

to serve
1 cucumber
smoked salmon
cod's roe

Preheat the oven to 180 °C (350 °F) and line the bottom and sides of a 33 cm x 23 cm Swiss roll tin with nonstick baking paper. Grease lightly with butter or margarine or spray with nonstick spray.

Squeeze any excess liquid from the spinach and chop finely. Process the spinach in a food processor along with the flour, nutmeg, chives and salt and pepper. When nearly smooth turn the mixture into a mixing bowl. Beat in the egg yolks. In a separate bowl whisk the egg whites until stiff peaks form and fold into the spinach mixture. Turn the mixture into the prepared baking sheet, spreading it out evenly. Bake for 20 minutes or until firm. Turn out onto a clean sheet of baking paper that has been lightly greased with nonstick spray and leave to cool.

Filling: Meanwhile beat the goat's milk cheese and cream cheese together. When the roulade has cooled to room temperature, spread the cheese mixture evenly on top and roll up. Wrap in a sheet of baking paper and then in foil and chill. Pack into the picnic basket along with the cucumber, salmon and caviar or cod's roe.

To serve: Remove the ends of the cucumber and, using a potato peeler, slice the cucumber into thin ribbons. Lightly roll up the ribbons and arrange on two plates. Slice the roulade and arrange two slices on each plate on top of the cucumber ribbons. Stack a little salmon on top and finish with a scoop of cod's roe.

Serves 4.

Hint
Cod's roe is affordable and available at most supermarkets.

Petits fours

Bake or buy a white sponge cake and cut it into squares. Spread each square with a thin layer of warmed smooth apricot jam. Roll out marzipan thinly and cover the top of each square with the paste. Make a fairly thick icing (the icing should fall off a spoon in a wide ribbon) with icing sugar, water and a little lemon juice and spoon on top of the cakes so it runs down the sides. (Colour the icing pink with a drop of red food colouring if desired.) Leave to set and decorate with the remaining icing. Arrange the petits fours in a foil container lined with baking paper.

spinach and goat's milk cheese roulade

Iced coffee

Add two scoops of ice cream, a few ice cubes, a little milk and a tot of liqueur to chilled strong filter coffee. Process in a food processor until smooth and serve with the shortbread.

Shortbread hearts

500 ml (2 c) cake flour
125 ml (½ c) icing sugar
30 ml (2 T) cornflour
1 ml (¼ t) baking powder
1 ml (¼ t) salt
250 g butter, diced
melted chocolate

Preheat the oven to 190 °C (375 °F) and line a baking sheet with baking paper.

Sift the cake flour, icing sugar, cornflour, baking powder and salt together. Gradually work in the butter, kneading until smooth. Roll out the dough to a thickness of 1 cm. Cut out heart shapes and prick all over the surface with a fork or skewer. Arrange on the baking sheet and bake for 25 minutes or until the shortbread turns golden. Leave to cool. Sprinkle sugar in the bottom of a cake tin and line with paper towels. Pack the shortbread into the tin. Dip the cooled shortbread into melted chocolate if desired.

Makes 25.

iced coffee with shortbread hearts

feast in the flowers

In Langebaan on the Cape West Coast flowers grow among the houses in cheerful profusion – a kaleidoscope of colour stretching to the horizon. This is where caterer Christine Capendale serves her festive spread to celebrate the season.

Menu
Fruit platter
Mini cheese loaves
Selection of spreads
Marinated olives and
 feta cheese with lemon

Lamb koftas with
 fig chutney
Spicy chicken kebabs
Olive and snoek tart

Instant lemon ginger beer
Hazelnut nougat

Fruit platter

Arrange any fresh fruit in season on a platter. Add cherry tomatoes on the vine and a bunch of spring onions for decoration. We chose pineapples, naartjies, kiwi fruit and strawberries.

mini cheese loaves

Mini cheese loaves

500 ml (2 c) cake flour
20 ml (4 t) baking powder
2 ml (½ t) salt
10 ml (2 t) sugar
2 ml (½ t) cayenne pepper
250 ml (1 c) grated
  Cheddar cheese
chopped chives
2 extra-large eggs
80 ml (⅓ c) oil
300 ml milk
grated Parmesan cheese

Preheat the oven to 180 °C (350 °F) and grease 6 muffin moulds or a muffin tin with 12 hollows thoroughly with butter or margarine or spray with nonstick spray.

Sift the cake flour, baking powder, salt, sugar and cayenne pepper together. Add the grated Cheddar and a little of the chopped chives. Beat the eggs, oil and milk together and add to the dry ingredients. Stir gently until the ingredients are just mixed. Spoon the dough into the muffin moulds or muffin tin and bake for 15 minutes or until done or when a skewer inserted into the centre of the bread comes out clean. Sprinkle with Parmesan cheese and chopped chives as soon as the loaves come out of the oven.

Serve with the spreads.

Makes 6 large mini loaves.

Selection of spreads

Biltong spread
Blend together 250 g cream cheese, 100 g finely shredded biltong and 5 ml (1 t) horseradish. Season with salt and pepper, adding a little cream if the mixture is too stiff. Spoon into a pâté dish and garnish with sliced biltong.

Roasted pepper spread
Core and quarter 2 red sweet peppers and place under the grill, skin side up. Grill until the skin is charred and begins to blister. Immediately place the peppers in a plastic bag and leave to cool. Rub off the skin and chop the peppers. Place in a food processor, add 5 ml (1 t) ground cumin, 5 ml (1 t) cumin seeds, 2 ml (½ t) ground coriander, 5 ml (1 t) paprika, 1 red chilli and 20 ml (4 t) balsamic vinegar. Season with salt and freshly ground black pepper to taste and process until smooth.

Makes about 150 ml.

Brie cheese spread
Slowly heat 125 g Brie with 50 g freshly grated Parmesan cheese and 50 ml crème fraîche until cheese has melted. Season with 2 ml (½ t) prepared mustard. Cool, then beat in another 100 ml crème fraîche. Season with black pepper. Spoon into a pâté dish and sprinkle with mustard powder.

Makes about 250 ml.

Marinated olives

Mix together 300 g mixed olives, 50 ml olive oil, 30 ml (2 T) balsamic vinegar, 1 garlic clove and 15 ml (1 T) brown sugar. Season with salt and pepper and add a few sprigs rosemary and thyme. Store in an airtight container.

Makes about 400 g.

Feta cheese with lemon

Mix 200 g feta cheese with the grated rind and juice of 1 lemon. Add 50 ml olive oil and season with chilli salt, freshly ground black pepper and a few sprigs thyme. Chill.

Makes about 250 g.

Spicy chicken kebabs

6 chicken breasts, boned
salt and pepper

basting sauce
80 ml (⅓ c) mayonnaise
10 ml (2 t) mild curry powder
5 ml (1 t) turmeric
30 ml (2 T) white wine
20 ml (4 t) chutney
20 ml (4 t) tomato paste
20 ml (4 t) sweet chilli sauce

Preheat the oven to 180 °C (350 °F) and grease a baking sheet well with oil, butter or margarine.

Cube the chicken breasts and thread them onto kebab skewers, taking care not to overload them. Season with salt and pepper. Blend the basting sauce ingredients and brush the kebabs with the mixture. Arrange the kebabs on the greased baking sheet and roast for 20 minutes, turning once halfway through the roasting time.

Serve hot or cold.

Makes about 12 kebabs.

Lamb koftas

500 g minced lamb
2 garlic cloves, crushed
60 ml (4 T) sesame seeds
50 ml finely chopped
  fresh coriander
salt and freshly ground black
  pepper to taste
5 ml (1 t) paprika
5 ml (1 t) ground cumin
3 ml (generous ½ t) ground
  coriander
½ medium onion, grated
1 thick slice white bread,
  soaked in a little milk
1 egg
flour
oil
20 kebab skewers

Turkish mince kebabs are traditionally served with lemon.

Preheat the oven to 180 °C (350 °F) and grease a baking sheet well with oil.

Mix all the ingredients except the flour and oil and roll into about 20 medium-sized balls. Roll each ball in flour and shape into a slight oval. Insert a kebab skewer in each ball and arrange on the baking sheet. Baste lightly with olive oil and roast for 30 minutes, turning once during the roasting time.

Serve with fig chutney (see recipe on page 94).

Makes 20 medium-sized meatballs.

spicy chicken kebabs

Fig chutney

Soak 100 g dried figs in 50 ml orange juice for 10 minutes. Add the grated rind of 1 orange and 2 cloves garlic, 125 g stoned dates and 1 small chopped green chilli. Place in food processor and pulse. Add 50 ml balsamic vinegar and 15 ml (1 T) olive oil. Process until smooth and well blended. Serve with lamb koftas.

Makes about 250 g.

Olive and snoek tart

5 sheets frozen phyllo
 pastry, thawed
50 ml melted butter
1 onion, finely chopped
1 green sweet pepper, seeded
 and finely chopped
20 ml (4 t) oil
250 ml (1 c) grated
 Cheddar cheese
500 ml (2 c) flaked
 smoked snoek
50 ml olive tapenade
250 ml (1 c) cream
50 ml milk
4 extra-large eggs
salt and pepper
15 stoned black olives

Preheat the oven to 180 °C (350 °F) and grease a 23 cm diameter pie dish with butter or margarine or spray with non-stick spray. Brush each sheet of phyllo pastry with the melted butter and stack the sheets on top of one another. Line the greased pie dish with the layered pastry.

Sauté the onion and green sweet pepper in the oil and mix with the cheese and snoek. Spread the bottom of the pastry shell with the olive tapenade and spoon the snoek mixture on top. Beat the cream, milk and eggs together. Season with salt and pepper and pour over the snoek mixture. Crumble the pastry slightly to neaten the edges. Bake for 30–35 minutes. Decorate the tart with black olives and serve hot or cold.

Makes 1 medium tart.

Instant lemon ginger beer

Place 80 g finely grated fresh ginger in a mortar with the grated rind of 2 lemons, juice of 1 lemon and 80 ml (⅓ c) honey or brown sugar. Mash with a pestle until the flavours are well-blended. Add 100 ml strong rooibos and leave to cool. Add 2 litres lemonade or ginger ale just before serving. Strain into a glass jug and serve with plenty of ice and garnished with mint leaves.

Makes 2 litres.

Hazelnut nougat

2 sheets rice paper
250 g sugar
100 ml honey
50 ml water
2 egg whites
250 g hazelnuts, toasted
  and skins removed
icing sugar and cornflour
  for dusting

Line a greased square or rectangular cake tin with one layer of rice paper. Slowly heat the sugar, honey and water in a small saucepan, stirring until the sugar has dissolved. Bring to the boil and simmer until the syrup reaches the hard-crack stage (150 °C to 152 °C). Do not stir but be careful not to let the syrup burn. Remove from the heat.

Meanwhile whisk the egg whites until they just form stiff peaks (don't overbeat). Gradually add the sugar syrup to the egg whites while beating. Beat until the mixture has cooled. Stir in the nuts and spoon the mixture onto the rice paper in the tin, spreading evenly. Cover with another sheet of rice paper and refrigerate for a few hours until firm. Cut into bars and dust with a mixture of icing sugar and cornflour. Wrap in cellophane and refrigerate.

Makes 16 bars.

hazelnut nougat

pack a picnic

Prepared everything at home, so that all you have to do is unpack and enjoy.

Spicy drumsticks with
chunky mayonnaise
sauce
Caprese loaf
Grilled brinjal and
tomato mould
Snoek quiche
Rum and raisin brownies

Caprese loaf

Spicy drumsticks

45 ml (3 T) fresh lemon juice
15 ml (1 T) Tabasco sauce
12 chicken drumsticks
45 ml (3 T) melted butter

crumb mixture
45 ml (3 T) finely chopped
fresh parsley
180 ml (¾ c) fine dry
breadcrumbs
pinch salt
15 ml (1 T) paprika
pinch cayenne pepper

The drumsticks are flavoured with Tabasco sauce for extra zip.

Mix the lemon juice and Tabasco sauce, brush the drumsticks with the mixture and chill. Mix all the ingredients for the crumb mixture. Brush the drumsticks with the melted butter and then roll in the crumb mixture. Chill for about 15 minutes.

Preheat the oven to 180 °C (350 °F). Arrange the drumsticks on a greased baking sheet and roast for about 40 minutes or until the drumsticks are golden brown and done. Leave to cool slightly before chilling in the refrigerator. Enjoy with chunky mayonnaise sauce.

Makes 12 drumsticks.

Chunky mayonnaise sauce

200 ml thick mayonnaise
60 ml (4 T) lemon juice
2 stalks celery, finely chopped
4 chives, finely chopped
30 ml (2 T) finely chopped
  fresh parsley
15 ml (1 T) whole-grain
  mustard
15 ml (1 T) tomato sauce
15 ml (1 T) Worcester sauce
4 garlic cloves, crushed
1 red chilli, seeded and
  finely chopped
5 ml (1 t) paprika
salt and freshly ground
  black pepper

Mix all the ingredients and chill until needed. Serve with spicy drumsticks (see recipe on previous page).

Caprese loaf

8 ripe tomatoes, thickly sliced
1 large chunk mozzarella
  cheese, thickly sliced
fresh basil leaves
2 Italian loaves, sliced
  diagonally but not
  right through
salt and pepper to taste

This is a sandwich version of the Italian Caprese salad. Pack the loaves whole – everyone then cuts his or her own sandwich.

Arrange a slice of tomato and mozzarella and a few basil leaves in the gap after every second slice of bread. Season with salt and freshly ground black pepper, wrap in cling film and chill. Serve with olive oil and balsamic vinegar.
  Makes 2 loaves.

Grilled brinjal and tomato mould

3 large brinjals, sliced into
  long strips
90 ml (6 T) olive oil
salt and freshly ground
  black pepper
4 tomatoes, cut in 3 mm
  thick slices
250 ml (1 c) olive tapenade
18 fresh basil leaves

Keep the mould cool for as long as possible and unmould it at the picnic spot. Serve, sliced, in pittas. The mould is not baked and therefore not that firm when sliced.

Heat the grill. Grease a nonstick loaf tin or oblong plastic container with oil. Brush or spray the brinjals with the olive oil and sprinkle with salt and pepper. Arrange in a single layer on baking sheets and grill for 3–4 minutes on each side or until golden brown but not crisp. Line the base and sides of the loaf tin or container with the grilled brinjal slices. Layer tomatoes on the base and spread over a layer of olive tapenade, followed by a layer of basil leaves. Cover with a layer of brinjal slices. Repeat the layers until all the ingredients have been used up. End with a layer of brinjals. Cover with cling film and chill for at least 4 hours but preferably overnight. Unmould on a plate just before serving and cut into thick slices.
  Serves 4–6.

Snoek quiche

crust
250 ml (1 c) cake flour
5 ml (1 t) dried or 15 ml (1 T)
  finely chopped fresh
  mixed herbs
250 ml (1 c) grated
  Cheddar cheese
125 g butter
45 ml (3 T) ice-cold water
  (optional)

filling
500 g smoked snoek, boned
  and coarsely flaked
250 ml (1 c) cherry
  tomatoes, halved
60 ml (4 T) finely chopped
  fresh parsley
250 ml (1 c) milk
3 extra-large eggs
salt and freshly ground
  black pepper

Pack the quiche in its dish into the picnic basket.

Preheat the oven to 200 °C (400 °F) and grease a 26 cm diameter loose-bottomed pie dish well with butter or margarine or spray with nonstick spray.

Place all the ingredients for the cheese crust in a food processor and process until well-blended. Remove from the bowl. Lightly gather into a ball and chill for 15 minutes. Press the dough into the base and up the sides of the pie dish. Neaten the edges and chill.

Arrange the snoek and tomatoes in the pie crust. Sprinkle with the parsley. Beat the milk and eggs together, season with salt and pepper and pour into the crust. Bake for about 40 minutes or until the filling has set and is done. Leave to cool in the pie dish and chill.

Makes 1 large tart.

Rum and raisin brownies

180 ml (¾ c) seedless raisins
125 ml (½ c) dark rum
200 g butter
125 g dark chocolate,
  coarsely chopped
500 ml (2 c) sugar
250 ml (1 c) cake flour
30 ml (2 T) cocoa powder
1 ml (¼ t) baking powder
4 extra-large eggs

Preheat the oven to 180 °C (350 °F) and grease a 20 cm x 20 cm square cake tin with butter or margarine or spray with nonstick spray. Line with baking paper and grease again.

Slowly heat the raisins and rum and simmer gently until most of the rum has evaporated. Set aside to cool. Gently heat the butter and chocolate until melted and smooth. Cool slightly. Pour into a mixing bowl and add the raisin mixture, sugar, cake flour, cocoa powder, baking powder and eggs. Mix well with a wooden spoon. Pour the mixture into the prepared cake tin, spread out evenly and bake for 50–60 minutes or until firm. Cool completely before slicing into squares. Cover and pack, in its tin, into the basket. Serve with coffee.

Makes 16 squares.

snoek quiche

teatime treats, for sharing

When the trees are bare, the last golden leaves of autumn are scattered on the ground, and the winter sun makes you pleasantly drowsy, it's time to invite your friends for tea and a chat. The first spring flowers will inspire you to serve tea in the garden on a table adorned with silver and fine porcelain. And a quick chat over a cup of coffee will do wonders for the soul.

stylish morning tea party

Anne Meyers, well-known author of the FOOD FOR LIFE recipe books, compiled a menu for a delicious selection of treats for a FAMSA morning tea in Stellenbosch. Hetta van Deventer of Laborie Restaurant in Paarl did the baking.

chicken and bacon terrine bites

Menu

Herby cheese bites
Hazelnut pâté and
  mushroom bites
Chicken and bacon
  terrine bites
Chilli tomato chutney
Pancakes with pesto,
  vegetable and feta filling
Thai-style potato bites
Butternut and piquanté
  pepper tartlets

Fruit tartlets
Tartlet shells
Meringue nests with
  caramel filling
Whole-wheat puffs
Pineapple and ginger filling

Herby cheese bites

10 slices brown bread,
  crusts removed
250 g fat-free smooth
  cottage cheese
250 g Cheddar cheese, grated
30 ml (2 T) hot English
  mustard
90 ml (6 T) finely chopped
  fresh parsley
30 ml (2 T) dried dill
1 bunch spring onions,
  chopped

Toast the slices of bread on 1 side only under the grill. Quarter each slice. Blend the remaining ingredients, reserving a third of the Cheddar cheese and spring onions for garnishing. Spread the untoasted sides of the slices of bread with the mixture. Place them on a baking sheet and sprinkle with the remaining cheese and spring onions. Grill for a few minutes or until the cheese mixture just begins to bubble. Garnish with slices of oven-roasted beetroot. Serve immediately.
  Makes 30–40 bites.

Hazelnut pâté and mushroom bites

10 slices brown bread,
  crusts removed
250 g mushrooms, sliced
little olive oil
salt
125 g toasted hazelnuts
250 g mascarpone cheese
250 ml (1 c) fresh basil leaves
1–2 garlic cloves
60 ml (4 T) melted butter
freshly ground black pepper
fresh herbs to garnish

Toast the slices of bread on 1 side only under the grill. Quarter each slice. Arrange the mushrooms on a baking sheet. Drizzle with olive oil and season with salt. Grill under the heated grill for a few minutes until done and leave to cool. Reserve 20 hazelnuts for garnishing. Process the remaining nuts with the cheese, basil, garlic and butter until smooth. Check seasoning and chill the pâté until firm (about 1 hour).

Just before serving, spread the untoasted side of each piece of bread with the pâté and arrange the grilled mushrooms on top. Garnish with ground black pepper, chopped nuts and sprigs of herbs.

Makes 40 bites.

Hint
Place the hazelnuts in a single layer on a baking sheet and toast for a few minutes in a hot oven until the skins are browned. Take care not to burn the nuts. Place on a clean, dry cloth and rub between your hands to remove the skins.

Chicken and bacon terrine bites

4 chicken breast fillets
125 ml (½ c) chicken stock
1 packet (250 g) bacon,
  rind removed
4 pork sausages,
  casings removed
1 can (410 g) low-fat
  evaporated milk
3 large eggs, whisked
125 ml (½ c) parsley sprigs
freshly ground black pepper
watercress or rocket

Serve these bites with chilli tomato chutney.

Preheat the oven to 190 °C (375 °F). Grease a 26 cm x 26 cm ovenproof dish with butter or margarine or spray with non-stick spray.

Poach the chicken breasts in the chicken stock for 5 minutes. Drain and roughly chop the chicken fillets. Place the meat in a food processor. Gently fry the bacon until lightly browned, remove with a slotted spoon and chop coarsely. Place in the food processor. Fry the sausage meat in the same pan until just done and place in the food processor. Add the evaporated milk, eggs and parsley to the meat, season to taste with pepper and process to the desired texture: smooth or coarse.

Spoon the mixture into the prepared dish and bake for about 40 minutes or until set. Remove from the oven, cut into squares and serve rocket and with chilli tomato chutney (see recipe on page 104).

Makes 24–30 squares.

Chilli tomato chutney

Heat a can of tomato jam and simmer for 5 minutes. Remove from the heat and add 10–30 ml (2–6 t) finely chopped seeded green chillies, 1–2 crushed garlic cloves and 60 ml (4 T) chopped chives. Cool and use as needed. Store leftover chutney in the fridge.

Pancakes with pesto, vegetable and feta filling

45 ml (3 T) olive oil
250 g cocktail tomatoes
500 g frozen French
  stir-fry mixture
125 ml (½ c) basil pesto
250 g feta cheese,
  coarsely crumbled
12 small, prepared pancakes,
  14–16 cm in diameter
bunch of chives
freshly ground black pepper

Heat the oil until very hot. Add the tomatoes and the stir-fry mixture and stir-fry over high heat for about 3 minutes or until just done. Remove from the heat and stir in the pesto and feta cheese. Spoon a little of the filling on each pancake, roll up and secure with chive strips. Season with pepper and, if necessary, place the serving platter in a hot oven for a few minutes before serving.

Makes 12 generous pancakes.

How to make pancakes

Sift 375 ml (1½ c) cake flour, 1 ml (¼ t) salt and 5 ml (1 t) baking powder together 3 times. Make a hollow in the centre. Beat 500 ml (2 c) water, 1 extra-large egg, 7 ml (1½ t) vinegar and 15 ml (1 T) oil together. Gradually add to the flour mixture and beat with a spoon or an electric mixer. Leave to rest for at least half an hour. Brush a 15 cm diameter pan with oil. Use a soup ladle and spoon only enough batter in the pan to cover the bottom. Tilt the pan, making sure that the batter is evenly spread. Flip and bake on other side till done.

Hint

These pancakes can be made ahead of time and frozen. Pack the pancakes between layers of wax paper in an airtight container and freeze. To thaw, place the pancakes on a plate and leave in the fridge until thawed.

pancakes with pesto, vegetable and feta filling and a selection of bread bites

Thai-style potato bites

1 kg frozen potato bites
oil for deep-frying
300–500 ml (1–2 c) Thai sweet
  chilli sauce
fresh coriander leaves

Deep-fry the potato bites in oil according to the packet instructions. Drain and arrange the bites on a baking sheet. Pour the sweet chilli sauce over the bites, mix well and bake in a preheated oven at 220 °C (425 °F) until the sauce has been absorbed and sticks to the bites. Place in small bowls and sprinkle with coriander. Serve with extra sweet chilli sauce.

Makes 36 bites.

Butternut and piquanté pepper tartlets

325 ml (1¼ c) peeled and
  diced butternut
20 ml (4 t) olive oil
4 leeks, sliced into rings
250 ml (1 c) piquanté
  peppers, thickly sliced
  into strips
1 batch (12) tartlet shells,
  prepared and left in the tin
  (see recipe on page 107, but
  omit the castor sugar for
  this recipe)
250 ml (1 c) evaporated milk
250 ml (1 c) cheese spread
250 ml (1 c) cream
4 large eggs, whisked
125 ml (½ c) finely chopped
  parsley, coriander or basil

Preheat the oven to 190 °C (375 °F).

Microwave, steam or cook the butternut until just done. Drain and set aside. Heat the oil and lightly stir-fry the leeks until browned. Divide the leeks, piquanté peppers and butternut among the tartlet shells. Heat the evaporated milk and add the cheese spread. Remove from the heat and beat until the cheese spread has melted. Cool slightly before adding the cream, eggs and herbs. Beat well and pour the mixture over the vegetables in the tartlet shells. Bake for 30–40 minutes or until the fillings have set. Cool and remove from the pans.

Makes 12 tartlets.

Fruit tartlets

egg custard
350 ml low-fat
  evaporated milk
1 large egg
2 egg yolks
20 ml (4 t) cake flour
20 ml (4 t) cornflour
60 ml (4 T) castor sugar
5 ml (1 t) vanilla essence

12 baked tartlet shells
  (see recipe on page 107)
500 g fresh fruit in season,
  peeled and sliced
a little extra castor sugar
125 ml (½ c) smooth
  apricot jam

Mix 60 ml (¼ c) of the evaporated milk with the egg, egg yolks, flour, cornflour and sugar. Heat the remaining milk and when it comes to the boil, beat in the egg mixture. Reduce the heat immediately and carry on beating until the mixture thickens. Remove from the heat and stir in the vanilla essence. Chill to room temperature and fill the tartlet shells with the filling. Sweeten the fruit to taste with extra castor sugar. Allow to stand for 30 minutes.

Arrange the fruit on top of the custard. Heat the jam and brush the fruit generously with the syrupy jam. Chill in the fridge for an hour before serving.

Makes 12 tartlets.

Tartlet shells

500 ml (2 c) cake flour
5 ml (1 t) salt
20 ml (4 t) castor sugar (omit
  for savoury shells)
175 g cold butter, diced
1 egg
5 ml (1 t) vinegar
15 ml (1 T) ice-cold water

Sift the cake flour, salt and castor sugar together. Rub the butter into the flour mixture until it resembles breadcrumbs. Whisk the egg, vinegar and cold water together and add to flour mixture. Lightly mix to form a dough. Wrap in cling film and refrigerate for at least 2 hours.

Roll out and line tartlet tins. Bake blind in a preheated oven for about 15–20 minutes or until shells are lightly browned and done. Leave to cool completely before removing from the tins.

Spoon a custard filling into the casings and decorate with fresh fruit in season. Alternatively, use for savoury tartlets.

Makes 12 tartlet shells.

How to bake blind

To bake blind means to bake a pastry case without a filling.

Line the tartlet tins with the pastry. Prick the bottom. Place a piece of baking paper over each tartlet and fill with a little rice or dried beans. Bake for about 10 minutes at 200 °C (400 °C), remove the baking paper as well as the beans or rice and bake for another 5–10 minutes until done, but not brown.

Meringue nests with caramel filling

1 can (397 g) caramel
  condensed milk
250 ml (1 c) cream
1 slab (100 g) milk chocolate,
  broken into squares
  and melted
30 ml (2 T) Cointreau
  (optional)
20 small (4–5 cm diameter)
  meringue nests

Beat the caramel condensed milk and cream together. Add the melted chocolate and Cointreau and continue beating until well blended. Chill. Fill the meringue nests with the caramel filling.

Makes 20 meringue nests.

meringue nests with caramel filling, and whole-wheat puffs

Whole-wheat puffs

30 ml (2 T) butter or
  margarine
30 ml (2 T) sunflower oil
1 ml (¼ t) salt
5 ml (1 t) castor sugar
250 ml (1 c) water
250 ml (1 c) cake flour
125 ml (½ c) bran
3 large eggs
1 egg white

Preheat the oven to 220 °C (425 °F) and grease a baking sheet with butter or margarine or spray with nonstick spray.

In a medium-sized saucepan, bring the butter or margarine, oil, salt, castor sugar and water to the boil. Add the flour and bran. Mix rapidly with a wooden spoon, beating the batter until it no longer sticks to the sides of the saucepan. Remove from the heat and leave the batter to cool for about 3 minutes.

Beat in the eggs one by one, ensuring each egg has been incorporated before adding the next. The mixture should be shiny. Beat the egg white until stiff and fold into the batter. Pipe or spoon 10–12 mounds of the batter at least 5 cm apart on a greased baking sheet. Bake for 20–25 minutes or until the puffs are lightly browned and dry to the touch when tapped. Switch off the oven and leave the puffs in the oven for another 15–20 minutes to allow them to dry out completely and retain their hollows. Using a sharp knife, cut a slit in the side of each puff and arrange them on a cooling rack to cool. Fill with the pineapple and ginger filling or whipped cream just before serving.

Makes 10–12 puffs.

Pineapple and ginger filling

300 ml finely grated
  fresh pineapple
10–20 ml (2–4 t) finely grated
  fresh ginger
4 cardamom seeds,
  slightly crushed
90 ml (6 T) brown sugar
125 ml (½ c) clear pineapple
  or apple juice
15–20 ml (3–4 t) cornflour
extra sugar and ginger
250 ml (1 c) stiffly
  whipped cream
1 batch whole-wheat puffs
icing sugar

Bring the pineapple, ginger, cardamom seeds, brown sugar and juice to the boil in a saucepan. Reduce the heat and simmer until the mixture has reduced and the pineapple is soft and cooked. Thicken the mixture with a little cornflour mixed to a paste with cold water. Add extra sugar and ginger if desired. Cool well and gently fold in the cream. Fill the puffs with the mixture and dust with hot chocolate powder or icing sugar before serving.

Makes 10–12 puffs.

garden tea party

Invite your friends to tea in the garden when the first spring flowers make their appearance.

Apple and cheese tartlets

crust
1 packet (200 g) coconut
  cookies, crushed
80 ml (⅓ c) melted butter
pinch ground cinnamon

filling
250 g creamed cottage
  cheese
200 ml castor sugar
1 can (385 g) pie apples,
  drained and puréed
grated rind of 1 small lemon
250 ml (1 c) cream
30 ml (2 T) gelatine
125 ml (½ c) dessert wine
  such as hanepoot or
  jerepigo
hundreds and thousands or
  cinnamon to decorate

Grease 25–30 small tartlet tins or one 20 cm diameter loose-bottomed cake tin with butter, margarine or nonstick spray.

Mix the ingredients for the crust and press into the base and sides of the tartlet tins or cake tin.

Filling: Beat the cottage cheese and sugar together until smooth. Add the apple purée and lemon rind. Whip the cream until stiff and fold into the mixture. Sprinkle the gelatine over the wine and leave it to sponge. Heat in the microwave oven or over hot water until dissolved and stir into the cottage cheese mixture. Spoon into the pie crusts and chill until set. Decorate with hundreds and thousands or dust with cinnamon.

Makes 25–30 tartlets or 1 large tart.

Chocolate cake with shocking pink icing

cake
1 extra-large egg
125 ml (½ c) cocoa, sifted
125 ml (½ c) oil
375 ml (1½ c) cake flour
5 ml (1 t) baking powder
5 ml (1 t) bicarbonate of soda
2 ml (½ t) salt
125 ml (½ c) buttermilk
5 ml (1 t) vanilla essence
250 ml (1 c) sugar
125 ml (½ c) water

pink chocolate icing
250 g white chocolate, broken
  into squares
250 ml (1 c) cream
15 ml (1 T) butter
drop red food colouring
desiccated coconut
berries or flowers

Preheat the oven to 150 °C (300 °F) and grease 2 x 20 cm diameter cake tins with butter or margarine or spray with non-stick spray. Line the tins with baking paper and grease again.

Place all the ingredients for the cake in a mixing bowl in the order they're listed, blending them only once the last ingredient has been added. Beat until smooth. Turn the batter into the prepared tins and bake for 30 minutes or until the cakes are done (a skewer inserted into the centre of the cakes should come out clean). Cool slightly in the tins before turning out onto a wire rack to cool completely. Cut each cake in half to form two thin layers if desired.

Slowly heat the chocolate and cream together until smooth. Remove from the heat and stir in the butter. Chill the icing until cold. Stir in a drop of red food colouring. Beat the icing until light and fluffy and use to sandwich the cake layers together. Reserve a little icing for covering the top and sides of the cake. Press coconut over the surface of the cake and decorate with berries or flowers.

Makes 1 medium cake.

apple and cheese tartlets

Pineapple cake

1 can (380 g) pineapple
 chunks
170 g soft butter
200 ml castor sugar
3 extra-large eggs
500 ml (2 c) self-raising flour
1 ml (¼ t) mixed spice
10 ml (2 t) baking powder
100 g ground almonds
icing sugar

A fruity cake that tastes even better if made in advance.

Preheat the oven to 180° C (350 °F) and grease an 18 cm square cake tin. Drain the pineapple chunks, reserving the syrup. Chop the fruit. Cream the butter and sugar together until light and beat in the eggs one by one. Add 45 ml (3 T) of the pineapple syrup and beat. Sift the flour, spice and baking powder on top of the butter mixture and mix in along with the pineapple and ground almonds. Turn the batter into the tin, spreading out evenly. Bake for an hour or until done (a skewer inserted into the centre of the cake should come out clean). Cool in the tin before turning out onto a wire rack. Dust with icing sugar. Cut into squares and serve with whipped cream.
 Makes 1 medium cake.

Sweet potato loaf cake

250 ml (1 c) yellow sugar
375 ml (1½ c) oil
4 extra-large eggs, separated
500 ml (2 c) cake flour
15 ml (1 T) baking powder
5 ml (1 t) ground cinnamon
5 ml (1 T) grated nutmeg
1 ml (¼ t) salt
180 ml (¾ c) peeled and
 grated sweet potatoes
100 g pecan nuts, chopped
180 ml (¾ c) desiccated
 coconut
5 ml (1 t) vanilla essence
100 ml coconut milk

icing
icing sugar
coconut milk
silver balls, hundreds and
 thousands or flowers

Preheat the oven to 180 °C (350 °F) and grease 2 x 1 litre loaf tins. Line the bottoms of the tins with baking paper and grease again.
 Beat the sugar and oil together. Add the egg yolks and beat. Sift the dry ingredients and spices over the oil mixture and stir in the sweet potatoes, pecan nuts, coconut, vanilla essence and coconut milk. Beat the egg whites until stiff and fold into the sweet potato mixture. Divide the batter between the 2 tins and bake for 50 minutes or until done (a skewer inserted into the centre of the cakes should come out clean). Cool before turning out onto a wire rack. Decorate with a slack runny made with sifted icing sugar and coconut milk. Silver balls, hundreds and thousands or flowers complete the picture.
 Makes 2 loaves.

Savoury treats

- Cut bread into cubes and spread with plain creamed cheese. Roll in fine biltong.
- Beat together a few teaspoonfuls of taramasalata, a chopped gherkin and a few spoonfuls smooth cottage cheese. Spread on toasted bread rounds.

ineapple cake

coffee culture

Few things lift your spirits quite as quickly as a steaming cup of good coffee, accompanied by a sweet treat. During our visit to the hospitable towns of Riversdale and Heidelberg in the Cape, we feasted on a wide selection of home-baked goodies.

Tritonia muffins
Instant scones
Chocolate mousse cake
Marbled cheesecake
Fridge cheesecake
Baked cheesecake
Lemon meringue
  ice-cream cake
Coffee cream tart
Nutty wafers
Tipsy tart
Choclate mousse tartlets

Tritonia muffins

750 ml (3 c) bran
250 ml (1 c) boiling water
250 ml (1 c) sugar
110 g butter or margarine
250 ml (1 c) cake flour
375 ml (1½ c) whole-wheat
  flour
2 ml (½ t) salt
12 ml (2½ t) bicarbonate
  of soda
60 ml (4 T) buttermilk
2 extra-large eggs, whisked

At the Tritonia coffee bar in Riversdale you can enjoy most of these cakes and tarts.

Preheat the oven to 180 °C (350 °F) and grease a muffin tin with 12 hollows well with butter or margarine or spray with nonstick spray. Mix together the bran, boiling water, sugar and butter. Leave to cool. Combine the cake flour, whole-wheat flour and salt. Add the bran mixture. Dissolve the bicarbonate of soda in the buttermilk, add the eggs and stir into the bran mixture. Spoon the mixture into the muffin tin hollows and bake for 15–20 minutes or until done.
  Makes 12 muffins.

Instant scones

Preheat the oven to 220 °C (425 °F) and grease a 20 cm rectangular tin with butter or margarine or spray with non-stick spray and dust with extra cake flour.

Lightly mix 4 x 250 ml (4 c) cake flour, 20 ml (4 t) baking powder and a pinch salt with 500 ml (2 c) milk and 50 ml oil and roll into 5 cm balls. Pack the balls close together in the greased tin and dust with extra cake flour. Bake for 12–15 minutes until done (a skewer inserted into the centre of the scones should come out clean). Cool, turn out and break into scones. Serve with butter and jam.

Makes 15 large scones.

Tritonia muffins and instant scones

marbled cheesecak

Chocolate mousse cake

cake
250 ml (1 c) castor sugar
4 extra-large eggs, separated
125 ml (½ c) oil
5 ml (1 t) vanilla essence
250 ml (1 c) cake flour
12 ml (2½ t) baking powder
pinch salt
125 ml (½ c) cocoa powder
125 ml (½ c) hot water

topping 1
1 packet (90 g) chocolate or
   caramel instant pudding
150 ml cold milk
150 ml cream, whipped

topping 2
1 packet (90 g) instant
   chocolate mousse
150 ml cold milk
100 ml cream, whipped

decoration
chocolate leaves

Preheat the oven to 180 °C (350 °F) and grease a 25 cm square cake tin with butter or margarine or spray with non-stick spray. Line with baking paper and grease again.

Beat the castor sugar and egg yolks until thick. Add the oil and vanilla essence and beat well. Sift together the flour, baking powder and salt. Blend the cocoa powder and hot water to form a paste. Add the dry ingredients to the egg mixture, alternating with the cocoa mixture. Beat the egg whites until stiff and fold into the batter. Turn the batter into the prepared tin and bake for 30–35 minutes until done (a skewer inserted into the centre of the cakes should come out clean). Cool the cake in the tin before turning out onto a wire rack to cool completely.

Beat together all the ingredients for topping 1 until the mixture begins to thicken. Spread over the chocolate cake and leave to set. Beat together all the ingredients for topping 2 until the mixture begins to thicken and spread over the first topping. Cool until set.

Decorate with the chocolate leaves and chill until needed. Makes 1 large cake.

How to make chocolate leaves
Spread melted chocolate over the backs of cleaned and dried rose leaves and leave to set. Carefully remove the leaves as soon as the chocolate has set.

Marbled cheesecake

1 packet (200 g) Tennis
   biscuits, crushed
60 ml (4 T) butter, melted
3 sachets (125 ml each)
   instant cream
375 ml (1½ containers)
   smooth cottage cheese
1½ cans (397 g each)
   condensed milk
10 ml (2 t) vanilla essence
180 ml (¾ c) fresh lemon juice
25 ml (5 t) gelatine
80 ml (⅓ c) boiling water
200 g dark chocolate, broken
   into squares
5 ml (1 t) milk
45 ml (3 T) coffee liqueur

Served at the Rooi Aalwyn stall in Riversdale.

Grease a 24 cm diameter loose-bottomed cake tin with butter or margarine or spray with nonstick spray.

Mix the crushed biscuits with the melted butter and press the mixture into the base of the cake tin. Whip the cream until stiff. Add the cottage cheese, condensed milk and vanilla essence and mix. Add the lemon juice and mix. Sprinkle the gelatine over the boiling water, stirring until dissolved. Add to the cottage cheese mixture and mix. Divide in half.

Heat the chocolate, milk and liqueur, stirring until the chocolate has melted. Stir the chocolate mixture into one half of the cottage cheese mixture. Turn the chocolate cheese mixture into the cake tin, alternating with the plain cheese mixture. Using a skewer, stir the mixture to create a marbled effect. Place in the fridge to set. Unmould onto a platter.

Makes 1 large cake.

Fridge cheesecake

2 packets (200 g each)
   Marie biscuits
120 g butter, melted
3 containers (230 g each)
   smooth cottage cheese
250 ml (1 c) sugar
2 tins (397 g each)
   condensed milk
20 ml (4 t) gelatine
150 ml lemon juice
750 ml (3 c) cream, chilled
granadilla pulp

Crush the Marie biscuits and mix with the melted butter. Press the biscuit mixture into the bottom of a 30 x 35 cm ovenproof dish. Beat together the cottage cheese, sugar and condensed milk until smooth.

In a small bowl, sprinkle the gelatine over the lemon juice and leave to sponge. Place the bowl with the sponged gelatine in a larger bowl of boiling water and leave until the gelatine has dissolved. Stir into the condensed milk mixture.

Whip the cream until stiff and fold into the condensed milk mixture. Pour over the biscuit crust and chill until set. Serve with granadilla pulp.

Makes 1 large cheesecake.

Baked cheesecake

crust
1 packet (200 g) Marie
   biscuits, crushed
60 ml (4 T) butter, melted

filling
3 containers (230 g each)
   creamed cottage cheese
4 extra-large eggs
250 ml (1 c) castor sugar
7 ml (1½ t) vanilla essence

Preheat the oven to 180 °C (350 °F). Grease a 25 cm diameter loose-bottomed cake tin with butter or margarine or spray with nonstick spray.

Mix the crushed biscuits with the melted butter and press the mixture into the base of the cake tin. Mix the remaining ingredients and pour over the base. Bake for 1 hour. Switch off the oven and leave to cool in the oven.

Makes 1 large tart.

Lemon meringue ice cream cake

1 can (397 g) condensed milk
200 ml lemon juice
finely grated rind of 2 lemons
500 ml (2 c) cream, chilled
30 small meringues

Adéle Wessels of Heidenberg made this frozen version of the well-known lemon meringue pie – it's perfect for a special occasion.

Line a 22 cm diameter spring-form cake tin with a double layer of cling film. Mix the condensed milk, lemon juice and rind. Whip the cream until stiff and fold into the mixture. Crush half the meringues and sprinkle in the bottom of the cake tin. Pour the condensed milk mixture on top. Arrange the remaining meringues on top. Cover and freeze overnight or until hard. Unmould and cut into slices. Serve with nutty wafers (see recipe on page 120).

Makes 1 medium cake.

emon meringue ice cream cake

Nutty wafers

6 extra-large egg whites
250 ml (1 c) castor sugar
250 ml (1 c) cake flour
150 g mixed nuts,
  coarsely chopped

Preheat the oven to 180 °C (350 °F) and grease a medium-sized cake tin with butter or margarine or spray with nonstick spray.

Whisk the egg whites until soft peaks form. Beat in castor sugar by the spoonful, beating continuously. Using a spatula, fold in cake flour and nuts. Pour the batter into the prepared tin and bake for 45–60 minutes. Leave to cool before slicing thinly, using a serrated knife. Arrange on a baking sheet in a single layer and dry out at 100 °C (200 °F).

Store in an airtight container.

Makes 25–30 wafers.

Coffee cream tart

cake
250 ml (1 c) sugar
4 extra-large eggs
pinch salt
375 ml (1½ c) cake flour
10 ml (2 t) baking powder
5 ml (1 t) instant
  coffee powder
30 ml (2 T) butter or
  margarine
60 ml (4 T) water
60 ml (4 T) milk
5 ml (1 t) vanilla essence

sauce
500 ml (2 c) water
310 ml (1¼ c) sugar
30 ml (2 T) instant
  coffee powder
45 ml (3 T) brandy
5 ml (1 t) vanilla essence

topping
1 can (380 g) caramel
  condensed milk
1 packet (90 g) instant
  caramel pudding
400 ml cold milk
1 container (250 ml) cream,
  whipped

Preheat the oven to 180 °C (350 °F). Grease a 25 cm x 30 cm ovenproof dish well with butter or margarine or spray with nonstick spray.

Beat the sugar and eggs until thick and pale and all the sugar has dissolved. Sift together the salt, flour, baking powder and instant coffee powder and fold into the egg mixture. Heat the butter or margarine, water and milk, remove from the heat and stir in the vanilla essence. Add to the flour mixture and mix. Turn the batter into the prepared dish and bake for 30 minutes or until pale brown and done (a skewer inserted into the centre of the cakes should come out clean).

Bring the water, sugar and coffee powder to the boil and boil rapidly for 2 minutes. Remove from the heat and stir in the brandy and vanilla essence. Prick the tart with a fork as soon as it comes out of the oven and pour the sauce over. Leave to cool.

Beat together the ingredients for the topping, except the cream, and pour over the tart. Chill until firm and decorate with the whipped cream.

Makes 1 large tart.

Tipsy tart

tart
250 g dates, finely chopped
5 ml (1 t) bicarbonate of soda
250 ml (1 c) boiling water
125 ml (½ c) butter or
  margarine
250 ml (1 c) sugar
2 extra-large eggs
500 ml (2 c) cake flour
5 ml (1 t) baking powder
3 ml (generous ½ t) salt
250 ml (1 c) chopped walnuts

syrup
310 ml (1¼ c) sugar
15 ml (1 T) butter
180 ml (¾ c) water
5 ml (1 t) vanilla essence
pinch salt
125 ml (½ c) brandy

Preheat the oven to 180 °C (350 °F) and grease 2 x 22 cm diameter pie dishes with butter or margarine or spray with nonstick spray.

Place the dates in a bowl, sprinkle with the bicarbonate of soda and pour over the boiling water. Stir and leave to stand until cool. Cream the butter and sugar until the mixture is pale and fluffy. Add the eggs one by one, beating well after each addition. Sift together the dry ingredients and coat the nuts with a little of the mixture. Add the dates to the butter mixture and fold in the dry ingredients, followed by the walnuts. Spoon the batter into the prepared pie dishes and bake for 30–40 minutes or until done (a skewer inserted into the centre of the cakes should come out clean).

Heat the sugar, butter and water until the sugar has dissolved. Bring to the boil and simmer for 5 minutes. Remove from the heat and add the vanilla essence, salt and brandy. Stir well and carefully pour over the tarts as soon as they come out of the oven. Cool slightly. Serve the tart with whipped cream.

Makes 2 medium tarts.

Chocolate mousse tartlets

crust
1 roll (200 g) frozen puff
  pastry, thawed
1 egg, whisked
10 ml (2 t) cinnamon sugar
3 ml (generous ½ t) mixed
  spice
finely grated rind of 1 lemon

mousse filling
160 g dark chocolate, broken
  into squares
125 ml (½ c) cream
30 ml (2 T) butter
50 ml cocoa powder
30 ml (2 T) castor sugar
250 ml (1 c) cream, chilled
chocolate curls and berries
  to serve

Adéle Wessels of Heidelberg (Cape) serves these tartlets as a sweet treat at the end of a special meal.

Preheat the oven to 200 °C (400 °F) and grease the outside of small dariole moulds with nonstick spray.

Roll out the puff pastry until slightly thinner, brush with the whisked egg and sprinkle with the cinnamon sugar, mixed spice and finely grated lemon rind. Roll up again and cut into 2 cm slices. Chill for 2 hours. Roll out the slices once more and cover each of the moulds with a piece of dough. Bake for about 10–15 minutes or until done and golden brown. Cool before carefully removing the moulds.

Heat the chocolate and 125 ml (½ c) cream in the microwave oven at 100 per cent power for 30 seconds, stirring occasionally until the chocolate has melted. Stir in the butter, cocoa powder and castor sugar and leave to cool. Whip the cream until stiff and fold in. Leave to cool until set. Spoon 2 large spoonfuls of the mousse into each tartlet shell just before serving and decorate each plate with chocolate curls and berries.

Makes 18 tartlets.

an African feast

With its vast plains, dense bush, desert sands, towering cliffs and storm-ravaged coastlines, the African landscape is endlessly fascinating – and impossible not to love. Stripped bare and windswept, or thickly wooded and humid, this is our beloved land where we can still breathe freely and where the local foods are just as richly varied as the inhabitants, climate and landscape.

alfresco in style

It's Africa at its best: a table set outdoors in the Little Karoo and gourmet fare prepared with local ingredients. The place? Sanbona, a game reserve in the mountains between Montagu and Barrydale in the Western Cape.

beetroot soup with coriander pesto

Menu

Beetroot soup with
  coriander pesto

Kudu carpaccio salad

Springbok fillet with
  biltong crust
Rack of lamb with tomato
  lentils and rosemary
  sauce

Sago pudding with
  cinnamon syrup
Almond tart

Beetroot soup with coriander pesto

4 large beetroot, scrubbed
2 onions, finely chopped
olive oil
250 ml (1 c) dry white wine
500 ml (2 c) vegetable stock
salt and pepper to taste
125 ml (½ c) plain yoghurt

pesto
2 packets (30 g each) fresh
  coriander
1 packet (100 g) cashew nuts
  or pine nuts
60-90 ml (4-6 T) olive oil
pinch salt

Place the beetroot in a saucepan and add enough water to cover. Bring to the boil and cook until soft. Allow to cool in the cooking liquid. Remove the skins and dice the beetroot. Set aside.

Slowly sauté the onions in a little olive oil until soft. Add the wine and boil rapidly until reduced by half. Add the vegetable stock and diced beetroot and bring to the boil. Season with salt and pepper, cool slightly and process in a food processor to obtain a fairly rough texture. Stir in the yoghurt. Spoon the soup into bowls and garnish with coriander pesto.

Wash the coriander and pat dry. Process with the nuts in a food processor until smooth. Add the olive oil via the spout and process until a smooth, thick sauce is formed. Season with salt and store in the fridge until needed.

Serves 6.

Kudu carpaccio salad

dressing
500 ml (2 c) balsamic vinegar
150 ml white sugar

salad
smoked kudu fillet
  (about 580 g)
mixed lettuce, bean sprouts,
  cherry tomatoes and
  onion rings
Parmesan cheese

Fairly moist biltong may be used instead of kudu fillet.

Slowly bring the vinegar and sugar to the boil and reduce to a third (the sauce will be fairly thick). Make sure it doesn't burn. Cool to room temperature.

Freeze the fillet and cut into paper-thin slices. Arrange lettuce leaves, bean sprouts, cherry tomatoes and onion rings on each plate. Surround with slices of meat and garnish with Parmesan cheese shavings. Drizzle with the dressing.

Serves 6.

Springbok fillet with biltong crust

1 springbok fillet (about 1 kg)
salt and freshly ground
  black pepper
100 ml cake flour
2 eggs, whisked
125 ml (½ c) ground biltong

Preheat the oven to 160 °C (325 °F). Season the fillet. Roll in the flour, then in the whisked eggs and finally in the ground biltong. Oven-roast for 15–20 minutes until brown on the outside but still pink inside. Take care not to overcook the meat. Wrap the fillet in foil and leave in the warming drawer for 10 minutes. Heat a griddle pan until smoking hot and char-grill the fillet. Carve and serve with caramelised onions (see recipe on page 126).

Serves 4–6.

Caramelised onions

6 onions, thickly sliced
olive oil
150 ml red wine vinegar
3 bay leaves
2 cloves
125 ml (½ c) sugar
100 ml red wine

Stir-fry the onions in a little olive oil until soft. Add the red wine vinegar, bay leaves, cloves and sugar. Bring to the boil, reduce the heat and simmer until the liquid has evaporated. Add the red wine and reduce until the mixture is syrupy.
    Makes about 300 ml.

Rack of lamb

1 rack of lamb (about 1 kg)
oil
salt and freshly ground
  black pepper
fresh rosemary sprigs

Preheat the oven to 160 °C (325 °F). Trim the bones using a sharp knife and wrap them in foil. Brush the meat with oil and season with salt, pepper and rosemary sprigs. Oven-roast for 20–25 minutes per 500 g. Leave for 10 minutes before carving into chops. Char-grill on a hot griddle pan. Serve with tomato lentils and rosemary sauce.
    Serves 6.

Rosemary sauce

Sauté 1 chopped onion in olive oil until soft. Add 40 ml (8 t) sugar and 200 ml red wine and bring to the boil. Add 400 ml beef stock. Strip the leaves off 3 sprigs of rosemary and add. Simmer until reduced and flavoursome.
    Makes about 500 ml (2 c).

Tomato lentils

Cook 200 g brown lentils in 500 ml (2 c) water until soft. Season with salt at the end of the cooking time, drain and set aside. Heat a little oil and fry 2 finely chopped onions until soft. Add 30 ml (2 T) red wine vinegar and simmer to reduce. Add 4 peeled, chopped tomatoes and the cooked lentils and season to taste with salt and freshly ground black pepper.
    Serves 4–6.

kudu carpaccio salad

Sago pudding

1 litre (4 c) milk
100 g butter
250 ml (1 c) sago
180 ml (¾ c) sugar
10 ml (2 t) vanilla essence
pinch salt
4 eggs, separated
60 ml (4 T) castor sugar

Preheat the oven to 180 °C (350 °F). Bring the milk, butter and sago to the boil. Reduce the heat and simmer the sago until cooked and transparent. Stir in the sugar, vanilla essence and salt. Add the egg yolks to the sago mixture, mix and spoon into an ovenproof-dish and bake for 20 minutes. Beat the egg whites and castor sugar until stiff and spoon on top of the baked sago. Bake for another 5–10 minutes. Serve with cinnamon syrup.
    Serves 4–6.

Cinnamon syrup

Slowly heat 250 ml (1 c) sugar, 4 cinnamon sticks and 250 ml (1 c) water until the sugar has dissolved. Bring to the boil and simmer until syrupy. Cool and remove the cinnamon sticks. Serve with sago pudding.

Almond tart

1 x 22 cm baked pie crust

filling
500 ml (2 c) sugar
125 ml (½ c) water
60 ml (4 T) honey
juice and finely grated rind of
  1 lemon
500 g flaked almonds

Only the crust of this easy-to-make tart requires baking.

Slowly heat the sugar, water, honey and lemon juice until the sugar has dissolved. Bring to the boil and simmer for 1–2 minutes until the mixture becomes syrupy. Stir in the lemon rind and almonds and turn the mixture into the baked pie crust. Leave to cool. Store in the refrigerator. Serve with ice cream.
    Makes 1 medium tart.

a freedom buffet

Lifestyle expert and interior designer David Strauss invited friends to a special buffet to celebrate the freedom brought about by democracy. Traditional favourites like Sunday's roast, roast potatoes and beetroot salad were given a new twist, and even the well-known three-bean salad was served in a different guise.

Marrakesh leg of lamb

Menu
Radishes with vodka and
  sea salt

Marrakesh leg of lamb with
  chimichurri
Three-bean salad
Roast beetroot with
  skordalia

Dessert buffet
Dom Pedro
Fresh fruit in white wine
  with mascarpone
Orange cake

Radishes with vodka and sea salt

2 bunches unblemished
  fresh radishes
Maldon sea salt
vodka

*Radishes dipped in vodka then in salt make a refreshing snack.
Cherry tomatoes can be given the same treatment.*

Clean the radishes (don't peel them) and leave about 1 cm
of the stems intact. Arrange in a serving bowl with small
bowls of salt and vodka on the side. Guests dip a radish in the
vodka, then in the salt and pop it into their mouths.
  Serves 6.

Marrakesh leg of lamb

spicy paste
5 ml (1 t) turmeric
15 ml (1 T) ground coriander
15 ml (1 T) ground cumin
  (jeera)
pinch ground cinnamon
pinch ground cloves
60 ml (4 T) olive oil
juice of 2 lemons
2 cloves garlic, crushed

meat
1 leg of lamb, about 2,5 kg,
  boned and butterflied
salt and freshly ground black
  pepper to taste
fresh coriander leaves,
  chopped

*Transform a traditional roast into an exotic dish bursting with
African flavours.*

Grind all the spices with a mortar and pestle. Add the olive
oil, lemon juice and garlic and mix to form a paste. Using a
small sharp-pointed knife, make small incisions all over the
leg of lamb and rub the paste into the meat, also pressing
some of the paste into the incisions. Place the leg in a large
freezer bag and marinate in the fridge for at least 4 hours and
preferably overnight.
  Preheat the oven to 160 °C (325 °F). Remove the leg from
the fridge and leave to reach room temperature. Place the
meat in a roasting pan, season with salt and pepper and
roast for about 1 hour or until brown on the outside, but still
pink inside. Rest for 15–30 minutes before carving into thin
slices. Garnish with fresh coriander and serve at room temperature with chimichurri.
  Serves 4–6.

Chimichurri

*Basil pesto has become somewhat old hat, so ring the chang-
es and serve this traditional Argentinian sauce with the leg
of lamb.*

Mix 30 ml (2 T) white wine vinegar, 50 ml sunflower or olive
oil, 45 ml (3 T) chopped flat-leaf parsley, 5 ml (1 t) oregano,
2 crushed garlic cloves, 5 ml (1 t) paprika and 1 chopped
green chilli. Chill overnight.
  Makes about 125 ml (½ c).

Three-bean salad

1 can (400 g) barlotti beans
1 can (400 g) chickpeas
1 can (400 g) kidney beans
2 garlic cloves, crushed
plenty of fresh sage
150 ml olive oil
1 plum tomato, chopped
30 ml (2 T) fresh lemon juice
salt and freshly ground
  black pepper
1 red onion, peeled and
  thinly sliced
chopped flat-leaf parsley

This old favourite is given a Mediterranean twist. Use canned beans to give yourself more free time.

Drain the beans and chickpeas and rinse well.

Stir-fry the garlic and sage in a little olive oil until fragrant. Add the tomato and half the chickpeas and simmer until tender. Remove from the heat and add the beans, remaining chickpeas, olive oil and lemon juice. Season well with salt and pepper and leave to cool. Add the onion and garnish with the parsley.

Serves 6.

Roast beetroot

2 bunches young beetroot
olive oil
3–5 ml (generous ½ –1 t)
  fennel or dill seeds
good-quality vinegar
sugar

The quivering beetroot mould we've become accustomed to is hardly welcome in the new regime – here the beetroot is freed from its old-fashioned jelly disguise.

Preheat the oven to 180 °C (350 °F).

Clean the beetroot without peeling them and leave 2 cm of the stems intact. Place them in a roasting pan and drizzle with olive oil. Scatter the seeds over the beetroot and roast until tender but still firm. Leave to cool and remove the skins. Keep the beetroot whole if small, otherwise cut into rough chunks. Sprinkle with olive oil, vinegar and sugar to taste.

Serves 6.

Skordalia

2 medium potatoes (about
  400 g uncooked)
4 slices white bread,
  crusts removed
6 garlic cloves, peeled
60 ml (4 T) olive oil
40 ml (8 t) lemon juice
salt and white pepper to taste

Skordalia from Russia replaces roast or mashed potatoes. Experiment with parsley, coriander leaves, chillies, chives, cumin and paprika to vary the flavours.

Boil the potatoes in their jackets until cooked. Pull the skins off while still warm and mash the potatoes.

Soak the bread for 2 minutes in cold water and squeeze out the water. Place the potatoes, bread and garlic in a food processor and process until smooth. Add the olive oil and lemon juice while the machine is running. Season with salt and pepper to taste.

Spoon into a small dish and serve with beetroot.

Makes about 500 ml (2 c).

Fresh fruit in white wine with mascarpone

875 ml (3½ c) sugar
1 bottle (750 ml) white wine
12 fresh nectarines or plums
fresh mint
1 container mascarpone

Canned fruit with evaporated milk has been the stand-by pudding for many years – but now we have progressed to fresh fruit with mascarpone.

Place the sugar in a saucepan. Add the wine and mix. Heat, stirring until the sugar has dissolved, taking care that it doesn't boil. Simmer slowly until syrupy – about 8 minutes.

Add the unpeeled fruit to the boiling syrup. Simmer for about 3–4 minutes on both sides.

Remove from the syrup and skin the fruit. Cool. Arrange on a serving platter and add some of the sauce as well as a few mint leaves. Serve with mascarpone in a separate dish.

Serves 6.

Dom Pedro

good-quality whisky
vanilla ice cream
plenty of walnut halves

South Africa's favourite steakhouse drink, called 'skolliesop' in the Saldanha Bay Hotel, is served the way it's enjoyed in Buenos Aires.

Pour a double tot of whisky into a thick-rimmed café glass. Add a generous scoop of ice cream and sprinkle liberally with walnuts. Serve with long-handled spoons.

Orange cake

cake
250 g butter
250 ml (1 c) castor sugar
3 extra-large eggs
10 ml (2 t) grated orange rind
500 ml (2 c) cake flour
10 ml (2 t) baking powder
2 ml (½ t) salt
5 ml (1 t) vanilla essence
60 ml (4 T) orange juice
80 ml (⅓ c) poppy seeds

syrup
180 ml (¾ c) orange juice
180 ml (¾ c) sugar
grated rind of 1 orange
a little sherry or liqueur

Cake doubles as dessert on the freedom buffet. Serve with kumquat preserve – it's not only for muffins and scones!

Preheat the oven to 180 °C (350 °F) and grease a 23 cm diameter ring tin well with butter or margarine or spray with nonstick spray.

Cream the butter and castor sugar. Add the eggs one by one, beating well after each addition. Add the remaining ingredients and mix. Spoon into the prepared tin and bake for about 1 hour or until a skewer inserted into the centre of the cake comes out clean.

Bring all the ingredients for the syrup to the boil and pour over the hot cake. Leave the cake to cool in the tin. Slice and arrange the slices on a cake stand.

Makes 1 medium cake.

fresh fruit in white wine with mascarpone

venison and other African-style foods

Season venison with the flavours of north Africa – cumin and coriander, paprika, mustard and chilli. Add mint, parsley, lots of garlic and lemon for a wonderfully fresh twist.

venison potjie

Venison
Venison potjie
Venison kebabs
African pie
Leg of venison with
  spice rub

Bread
Rye bread
Unleavened loaves

Salad
Chakalaka
Banana and lentil salad
Beetroot and carrot salad

Venison potjie

125 ml (½ c) cake flour
10 ml (2 t) mustard powder
pinch ground cumin
7 ml (1½ t) dried thyme
2 kg venison shanks such
    as warthog, marinated
    overnight in 500 ml (2 c)
    buttermilk
salt
60 ml (4 T) oil
1 packet (125 g) bacon
10 whole pickling
    onions, peeled
6 garlic cloves
2 oranges (unpeeled), cut into
    segments
250 ml (1 c) white wine
1 small can (65 g) tomato
    paste
juice and rind of 2 oranges
a few sprigs lemon thyme
3 bay or lemon leaves
brown sugar to taste
30 ml (2 T) Dijon mustard
375 ml (1½ c) vegetable stock
30–45 ml (2–3 T) plain
    yoghurt

gremolata
finely chopped parsley
finely grated lemon rind
1–2 garlic cloves,
    finely chopped

The orange peel imparts a slightly bitter tang; peel the oranges if you prefer.

Combine the cake flour, mustard, cumin and thyme. Season the shanks with salt and roll in the flour mixture. Heat the oil in a black cast-iron pot and brown the shanks, a few at a time. Remove the meat from the pot and wipe it clean. Add a little more oil and stir-fry the bacon, onions, garlic and orange segments until lightly browned. Remove the orange segments and onions from the pot. Blend the white wine with the tomato paste and orange juice and rind and add to the pot. Reduce slightly. Return the meat to the pot and add the lemon thyme sprigs and bay or lemon leaves. Season to taste with a little brown sugar and Dijon mustard. Cover, reduce the heat and simmer until the meat is nearly tender, about 3 hours. Add the vegetable stock as needed. Return the orange segments and onions to the pot about half an hour before the end of the cooking time and simmer until the sauce is fragrant and slightly reduced. Stir in the yoghurt just before serving. Mix the chopped parsley, rind and garlic and scatter on top. Serve with putu pap.
   Serves 8.

How to make putu pap (crumbly porridge):
Bring 500 ml (2 c) water and 3 ml salt to the boil in a saucepan. Add 500 ml (2 c) mealie meal to the boiling water so it forms a heap in the middle of the saucepan. Do not stir. Cover and cook over low heat for about 10–15 minutes or until the mealie meal forms a skin on top. Stir with a fork until the mealie meal is loose and crumbly. Cover and heat for another 15–30 minutes. Stir once more until crumbly.
   Serves 4.

Venison kebabs

1,5 kg venison sausage,
  twisted into small pieces
250 g streaky bacon rashers
1 packet (250 g) pitted prunes
30 whole pickling onions
30 dried apricots

marinade
250 ml (1 c) olive oil
2 garlic cloves, crushed
a few sprigs lemon thyme
100 ml soy sauce
25 ml (5 t) brown vinegar
5 ml (1 t) mustard powder
pinch brown sugar
pinch fresh cumin

Our butcher made eland sausages for these kebabs. For a real African feast serve the kebabs with griddle cakes.

Wrap the pieces of venison sausage in the bacon rashers. Thread onto skewers with the prunes, pickling onions and apricots. Blend the ingredients for the marinade and marinate the kebabs in the fridge for at least 2 days. Cook over hot coals until just done.

Makes about 15–20 kebabs.

African pie

chermoula
180 ml (¾ c) lemon juice
20 ml (4 t) balsamic vinegar
125 ml (½ c) olive oil
125 ml (½ c) finely chopped
  fresh parsley
4 garlic cloves, crushed
15 ml (1 T) paprika
10 ml (2 t) ground cumin
2 ml (½ t) chilli powder

filling
1,5 kg venison such as
  springbok, cubed
500 g stewing lamb
250 g back bacon, cut
  into pieces
2 onions, sliced into rings
2 garlic cloves, crushed
375 ml (1½ c) water
salt
125 ml (½ c) red wine
125 ml (½ c) white wine
15 ml (1 T) cake flour
15 ml (1 T) apricot jam
1 roll phyllo pastry

Bake a venison pie flavoured with chermoula, a truly African spice mix.

Mix all the ingredients for the chermoula. Place the meat in a nonmetallic dish and pour the chermoula over. Cover and refrigerate for 12 hours.

Fry the bacon, onions and garlic in a pressure cooker until done. Add the marinated meat and brown slightly. Add the remaining chermoula marinade and water and bring to the boil. Season with salt, cover with the pressure cooker lid and heat. When the cooker reaches full pressure, reduce the heat and pressure-cook the meat until it falls off the bone. Leave to cool slightly and remove the bones. Blend the wine with the cake flour and add to the meat along with the jam. Bring to the boil and cook until fragrant. Cool.

Preheat the oven to 200 °C (400 °F). Grease a large pie dish with butter or margarine or spray with nonstick spray. Line with 6–8 sheets of phyllo pastry, each sprayed with nonstick spray. Leave the pastry to hang over the sides of the dish. Spoon the meat into the pastry case and fold the pastry sides over the meat mixture. Decorate with the remaining phyllo pastry. Spray with nonstick spray and bake until the filling is heated through and the pastry is pale brown. Serve with chakalaka (see recipe on page 142) on the side.

Makes 1 large pie.

African pie

Leg of venison with spice rub

2 kg leg of venison such as
    springbok
lardons, bacon rashers and
    garlic strips

spice rub
250 ml (1 c) finely chopped
    mint leaves
60 ml (4 T) lemon juice
60 ml (4 T) olive oil
2 garlic cloves, crushed
30 ml (2 T) ground coriander
10 ml (2 t) ground cumin
10 ml (2 t) paprika
5 ml (1 t) chilli powder
salt

The venison leg is rubbed with a mixture similar to North African harissa rub. If you like it hot add a few finely chopped chillies. The leg can also be cooked over medium-hot coals, in which case it must be covered while cooking. As the meat crisps on the outside, feel free to cut off a piece and sample the delights to come.

Mix all the ingredients for the spice rub. Make incisions all over the surface of the leg of venison and stuff with the lardons (strips of fat for larding), bacon and garlic. Rub the spice rub into the leg and place it in a nonmetalic dish. Leave to marinate in the fridge for 2 days.

Preheat the oven to 160 °C (325 °F). Place the leg on the rack of a roasting pan, cover with aluminium foil and oven-roast for 20–25 minutes per 500 g meat plus 25 minutes extra. Brush frequently with the remaining spice rub. Serve with couscous, oven-roasted pumpkin slices and plain yoghurt seasoned with a pinch of cumin and chopped mint.

Serves 6–8.

Rye bread

4 x 250 ml (4 c) rye flour
2 x 250 ml (2 c) whole-wheat
    flour
10 ml (2 t) salt
1½ packets (10 g each)
    instant yeast
30 ml (2 T) oil
5 ml (1 t) honey
500 ml (2 c) lukewarm water
rye flour for dusting

This flop-proof recipe comes from Caryl Vaughan-Scott's book Whole Energy – Wholesome Healthy Cooking.

In a large mixing bowl sift the rye flour, whole-wheat flour and salt together. Add the instant yeast and mix by hand. Mix the oil, honey and lukewarm water and add to the dry ingredients, again mixing by hand to form a dough. Knead well until the dough becomes elastic and leaves the sides of the bowl. Add a little more lukewarm water or a little more flour as needed. Cover the bowl with cling film and leave to rise in a warm place until doubled in size.

Remove the dough from the bowl and knock back on a floured surface. (If the dough is sticky, dust with a little rye flour.) Divide the dough in 2, shape into ovals, dust well with rye flour and cut a few slashes in the top of the loaves. Set the loaves on greased baking sheets and place in a cold oven. Turn the oven on to 190 °C (375 °F) and bake the loaves for about 1 hour or until they sound hollow when tapped lightly on the base. Serve with butter and cheese.

Makes 2 medium loaves.

Unleavened loaves

875 ml (3½ c) cake flour
2 ml (½ t) salt
250 ml (1 c) lukewarm water

topping
cream cheese
pickled onions

This bread is made without a rising agent. In Namibia I ate it with sour cream and finely chopped hard-boiled eggs. When we tested the recipe we discovered a bottle of pickled onions in the fridge. The unleavened loaves were simply delicious served with cream cheese and the pickles.

Preheat the oven to 200 °C (400 °F). Dust a baking sheet with a little flour.

Sift the flour and salt together and add just enough water to form a firm dough. Knead well until the dough becomes smooth and elastic and leaves the sides of the bowl. Add a little more lukewarm water or a little more flour as needed. Cover with cling film and leave to rest for half an hour (this makes it easier to roll out).

Divide the dough into 16 uniform pieces and roll out each piece into a 3 mm thick rounds on a floured surface. Place the rounds on the prepared baking sheet and bake for about 10–12 minutes or until pale brown and slightly puffed up. Serve with cheese and pickles or green fig preserve.

Makes 16 loaves.

Hints

- Instant yeast is not sponged beforehand, but added directly to the flour. A further advantage is that the dough must rise properly the second time only, while about 10 minutes is sufficient for the first rising.
- Ensure that the water or other liquid is neither too cold nor too hot. If it's too cold it won't activate the yeast responsible for the rising process and if it's too hot it will kill it off. A good way to test the temperature is if you can keep your hand in the liquid without burning yourself. Add all the liquid as indicated; if the dough is too slack it's preferable to add more flour rather than adding more liquid to a mixture that's too dry.

Chakalaka

1 onion, sliced
2 garlic cloves, crushed
1–2 chillies, seeded and
  finely chopped
125 ml (½ c) olive oil
1 green sweet pepper, seeded
  and sliced into strips
1 yellow sweet pepper,
  seeded and sliced
  into strips
500 g cabbage, shredded
500 g carrots, grated
15 ml (1 T) cayenne pepper
15 ml (1 T) paprika
1 can (410 g) peas, drained
salt and black pepper

This traditional African dish is delicious with any kind of meat or stews.

Sauté the onion, garlic and chillies in half the oil until soft. Add the sweet peppers and stir-fry for another 2–3 minutes. Add the cabbage and carrots along with the cayenne pepper, remaining oil and paprika and stir-fry until the vegetables are cooked but still firm. Add the peas and mix. Season with salt and pepper. Remove from the heat and leave so the flavours can develop. Serve hot or cold.
  Serves 6.

chakalaka

Banana and lentil salad

400 g brown lentils
salt

45 ml (3 T) oil
1 onion, chopped
1 red sweet pepper, seeded
    and sliced into strips
15 ml (1 T) crushed garlic
3–4 bananas, sliced
60 ml (4 T) balsamic vinegar
45 ml (3 T) finely chopped
    fresh coriander
30 ml (2 T) finely chopped
    fresh parsley
salt and freshly ground
    black pepper

A delicious combination.

Rinse the lentils and place them in a saucepan. Cover with water and cook until soft. Add salt at the end of the cooking time. Drain and set aside.

Heat the oil in a frying pan and stir-fry the onion, red sweet pepper and garlic until cooked. Add to the lentils along with the remaining ingredients, mixing carefully. Season with salt and pepper if necessary.

Serves 6–8.

Beetroot and carrot salad

1,5 kg beetroot, leaves intact
45 ml (3 T) olive oil
4–6 carrots, scraped and cut
    into pieces

dressing
125 ml (½ c) olive oil
75 ml (5 T) lemon juice
6 chives, chopped
15 ml (1 T) cumin (jeera)
15 ml (1 T) paprika
1 garlic clove, crushed
3 ml (generous ½ t) honey
salt and freshly ground
    black pepper

Preheat the oven to 200 °C (400 °F). Arrange the beetroot in an ovenproof dish and coat with the olive oil. Cover and roast for 2 hours or until tender, removing the cover halfway through the roasting time. Leave until cool enough to handle and remove the skins. Cut the flesh into pieces.

Arrange the carrot pieces in a separate ovenproof dish and roast until just tender. Arrange the beetroot and carrots in a salad bowl. Blend all the ingredients for the salad dressing and drizzle over the vegetables. Serve hot or cold.

Serves 6.

out on

the stoep

Every house ought to have a cosy stoep or outdoor area where a trestle table or large kitchen table can be used for lazy late-afternoon get-togethers, fashionable cocktail functions or a brunch with friends. Show your originality by draping the table with scarves and cloths, and using fun combinations of cutlery and crockery in the settings. Invite everyone, including the pets, to join in the gathering.

breakfast for late risers

Well-known entertainment chef Francois Ferreira set a table on the stoep and invited friends to brunch. No late riser can resist such a spread.

rooibos punch

Menu
Rooibos punch

Herb quiche with
  sun-dried tomatoes
Mixed mushroom quiche
Haddock quiche with
  pepper sauce
Herbed baby
  marrow terrine
Mixed vegetable terrine
  with onion marmalade
Herb salad with fynbos
  vinaigrette
Marinated ostrich terrine

Lemon mousse
Yashini's trifle

Rooibos punch

500 ml (2 c) strong rooibos
  tea
1 litre (4 c) mango juice
a few lemon slices
mint leaves
dry sparkling wine or soda
  water to taste

Leave the rooibos tea to cool, then mix with the mango juice. Add the lemon slices and a few mint leaves. Chill and add sparkling wine or soda water just before serving.

Herb quiche with sundried tomatoes

6 garlic poppadums
3 sun-dried tomatoes, chopped
15 ml (1 T) chopped fresh herbs such as basil, oregano and marjoram
180 ml (¾ c) grated white Cheddar cheese
2 large eggs
300 ml milk
salt and pepper to taste

Francois uses poppadums for crusts when making individual quiches – they work like magic.

Preheat the oven to 180 °C (350 °F). Plunge the poppadums into boiling water for a few seconds to make them pliable. Line each of 6 greased tartlet tins with a poppadum, then sprinkle a layer of tomatoes, herbs and cheese in the bottom of each tin. Whisk the eggs and milk together and season with salt and pepper. Pour the mixture into the tins and bake for 15–20 minutes or until the filling has set. Serve lukewarm with salad.
    Makes 6 quiches.

Mixed mushroom quiche

6 cumin poppadums
6 Portabellini mushrooms, sliced
6 button mushrooms, sliced
6 oyster mushrooms, sliced
2 large eggs
300 ml plain yoghurt
salt and black pepper to taste
180 ml (¾ c) grated yellow Cheddar cheese

Preheat the oven to 180 °C (350 °F). Plunge the poppadums into boiling water for a few seconds to make them pliable and use to line greased aluminium foil tartlet tins. Place a few slices of each kind of mushroom in the bottom of each shell with the oyster mushrooms on top. Whisk together the eggs and yoghurt, season with salt and pepper and pour into the tartlet shells. Sprinkle with cheese and bake for 15–20 minutes or until done. Serve lukewarm with salad.
    Makes 6 quiches.

Haddock quiche

6 plain poppadums
600 g smoked haddock,
  skin removed
1 onion, chopped
75 g butter
130 ml flour
300 ml milk
2 eggs, whisked
salt and pepper
breadcrumbs and grated
  Parmesan cheese
  for sprinkling

Preheat the oven to 180 °C (350 °F). Plunge the poppadums into boiling water for a few seconds to make them pliable. Line individual aluminium foil tartlet tins with a poppadum each. Steam the fish and flake. Fry the onion in butter, add the flour and mix. Add the milk, stirring continuously until the sauce thickens. Add the fish, season and cool. Add the eggs, season with salt and pepper and spoon the mixture into the poppadum shells. Sprinkle with breadcrumbs and Parmesan cheese. Bake for 15–20 minutes or until the filling has set. Serve lukewarm with red pepper sauce.

Makes 6 quiches.

Red pepper sauce

Roughly chop 2 red sweet peppers and sauté in a little oil until soft, along with a few garlic cloves. Season with salt and pepper and add about 50 ml olive oil and 25 ml (5 t) verjuice (green grape vinegar). Process in a food processor until blended but still fairly coarse.

Herbed baby marrow terrine

1 kg fresh baby marrows
15 ml (1 T) salt
50 g butter
4 large eggs
300 ml thick cream
30 ml (2 T) chopped fresh
  herbs such as parsley,
  oregano and sage
pinch cayenne pepper
freshly ground black pepper

This terrine can also be made 1–2 days in advance. Serve with onion marmalade (see recipe on page 152).

Preheat the oven to 180 °C (350 °F). Grease a small aluminium foil loaf tin with butter or margarine or spray with nonstick spray. Line with wax paper and grease again.

Grate the baby marrows, sprinkle with salt and leave to stand for 1 hour. Drain and discard the liquid. Rinse the marrows under running water and pat dry.

Melt the butter and, stirring continuously, stir-fry the grated marrows for 10 minutes or until soft. Leave to cool. Whisk together the eggs and cream and add the herbs, seasoning and baby marrows. Mix well and spoon into the prepared tin. Cover and place in an ovenproof dish filled halfway with hot water. Bake for 1¼ hours until firm. Leave to cool and chill.

Serves 4–6.

haddock quiche with red pepper sauce

mixed vegetable terrine

Mixed vegetable terrine

500 g carrots, scraped and
    finely chopped
1 onion, chopped
100 g butter
500 g fresh spinach, rinsed
    and stems removed
250 ml (1 c) grated white
    Cheddar cheese
500 g Portabellini
    mushrooms, sliced
750 ml (3 c) white sauce
3 large eggs
salt and pepper

Serve with fynbos vinaigrette.

Preheat the oven to 180 °C (350 °F) and grease 2 small aluminium foil loaf tins well with butter or margarine or spray with nonstick spray.

Sauté the carrots and onion in a third of the butter until soft. Set aside. Chop the spinach and sauté in another third of the butter until wilted. Add the cheese to the spinach while hot. Sauté the mushrooms in the remaining butter until soft. Mix a third of the white sauce with each of the vegetables. Add an egg to each of the vegetables and mix. Season with salt and pepper. Mix. Spoon the carrots into the tin, followed by the spinach and the mushrooms. Cover with aluminium foil and place the tin in an ovenproof dish filled halfway with hot water. Bake for 1½ hours or until firm. Cool in the tin and chill overnight.

Serves 6–8.

Herb salad

Prepare an individual salad for each guest. Insert a bunch of herbs into a pasta tube, e.g. cannelloni, so guests can use whatever they like.

Fynbos vinaigrette

Mix 75 ml (5 T) olive oil (or a mixture of olive and canola oils), 75 ml (5 T) white wine vinegar, 5 ml (1 t) sugar, 5 ml (1 t) prepared whole-grain mustard, salt and pepper to taste and 5 ml (1 t) each finely chopped wild sage, rosemary and garlic. Use as a salad dressing and to serve with the vegetable terrine.

Hint

For a tasty addition to the salad, place thick slices of red onion in a jar and fill with Cinzano. Store in the fridge (not at room temperature) and use in any salad. The onions will keep well for about a month.

Onion marmalade

Place 2 sliced onions, 15 ml (1 T) mustard seeds, 125 ml (½ c) balsamic vinegar, 125 ml (½ c) water and 125 ml (½ c) white sugar in a saucepan and bring to the boil. Reduce the heat and simmer until the liquid has reduced and formed a thick syrup.

Serve at room temperature with the herbed baby marrow terrine (see recipe on page 148).

Marinated ostrich terrine

marinade
1 carrot, finely chopped
1 shallot or leek, finely
  chopped
15 ml (1 T) olive oil
250 ml (1 c) red wine vinegar
freshly ground black pepper
1 sprig each sage and parsley
bay leaves

meat mixture
500 g boned ostrich meat
1 packet (250 g) streaky
  bacon
2 packets (500 g) shoulder
  bacon
250 g ostrich liver, cleaned
1 onion, chopped
1 shallot or leek, chopped
1 egg, lightly whisked
30 ml (2 T) cake flour
salt to taste
5 ml (1 t) freshly ground
  black pepper
5 ml (1 t) fresh or dried thyme
2 ml (½ t) crushed bay leaf
2 ml (½ t) ground cloves
1 thick slice white bread,
  crusts removed
150 g button mushrooms,
  finely chopped
20 g butter
5 ml (1 t) lemon juice

Make this terrine one day in advance so the flavours can develop. Francois served the terrine with smoked tomatoes.

Lightly stir-fry the carrot and shallot in the oil until soft. Add the remaining marinade ingredients and simmer for 10 minutes. Leave to cool.

Place the ostrich meat in the marinade and leave to marinate for 24 hours.

Preheat the oven to 180 °C (350 °F) and line 3 small aluminium foil loaf tins with the streaky bacon rashers so they overlap the sides of the tins.

Drain the ostrich meat, reserving the liquid. Place the ostrich meat, shoulder bacon, ostrich liver, onion and shallot in a food processor and process until the mixture is well blended but still slightly coarse. Add the egg, flour, seasoning and spices and mix. Soak the bread in the marinade liquid and add to the meat mixture. Mix well. Leave for 30 minutes.

Sauté the mushrooms in the butter along with the lemon juice and add to the meat mixture. Spoon the meat mixture into the bacon-lined tins and press down firmly. Fold the overlapping bacon rashers back over the meat. Cover the tins with a sheet of aluminium foil and place in an ovenproof dish filled halfway with hot water. Bake for 1½ hours or until done. Leave to cool in the loaf tins and place in the fridge. Turn out onto a serving platter and slice.

Serves 6 as a main course or 8–10 as a starter.

How to make smoked cherry tomatoes

Line the bottom of a black pot with aluminium foil. Scatter 250 ml (1 c) loose dried rooibos leaves on top and sprinkle with a little water. Place a cake rack over the leaves and arrange the cherry tomatoes on the rack. Cover with the lid of the pot and cover the lid with aluminium foil. Place the pot on the stove and heat until smoking. Turn off the heat and leave the pot on the stove for 5 minutes. Remove and leave to cool. Moisten the tomatoes with a mixture of olive oil and white vinegar.

lemon mousse

Yashini's trifle

Lemon mousse

10 ml (2 t) gelatine
45 ml (3 T) water
3 extra-large eggs, separated
150 g castor sugar
juice and finely grated rind of
  2 lemons
250 ml (1 c) thick cream,
  lightly whipped

Francois serves this dessert with deep-fried lemon rind.

Sponge the gelatine in the water for 10 minutes. Whisk together the egg yolks and castor sugar until thick and pale yellow. Add the lemon juice while beating, then the lemon rind. Heat the gelatine until dissolved but do not bring to the boil. Add to the egg yolk mixture and mix lightly. Leave until the mixture begins to set.

Beat the egg whites until soft peaks form and gently fold into the egg yolk mixture along with the cream. Spoon the mixture into small cups or into a dish and chill until set, about 4–5 hours. Decorate with deep-fried lemon rind.

Serves 6.

To make deep-fried lemon rind

Remove the rind with a zester. Sprinkle with castor sugar and leave to stand for 30 minutes. Remove from the syrup that has formed and deep-fry in hot oil until crisp. Scatter over the mousse.

Yashini's trifle

An exotic trifle served in glasses and dead easy to make.

Use 1 large strawberry per glass and cut into 5 slices. Arrange in the bottom of each glass. Sprinkle with a few almonds and grated dark cooking chocolate. Spoon a scoop of ice cream on top. Make a quick chocolate sauce or use a commercial sauce and spoon over the ice cream. Make a Chantilly yoghurt by mixing plain yoghurt with a little castor sugar and vanilla essence and spoon over the ice cream. Decorate with fresh or frozen berries.

braai in gourmet style

The boys' braai has been given a new twist by Tracy Foulkes and Paula Nel, the chefs in the TV food series THE GOURMET GIRLS. They serve their delicious fare in a cosy corner next to the house.

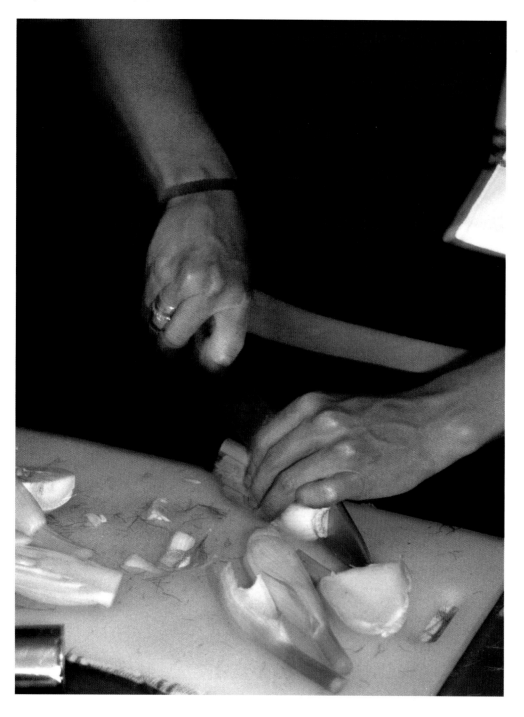

Red fish with gremolata

1 red roman or red
  stumpnose
extra-virgin olive oil
freshly ground salt and
  black pepper

gremolata
1 bunch Italian parsley
½ bunch mint
½ bunch lemon thyme
3 cloves garlic
2 pieces chopped lemon
  preserve (available
  from delis)
olive oil to taste
salt and pepper to taste

*Fish is delicious braaied over the coals. Tracy and Paula serve it
with baby potatoes and caramelised lemons.*

Keeping the head and tail intact, remove the scales and clean
the fish inside. Pat dry with paper towels. Rub the skin and
cavity with oil and season well. Cut three diagonal slashes
through the flesh, to the bone. Place all the ingredients for
the gremolata in a food processor and process until blended
but still coarse. Stuff the slashes and cavity of the fish with
the gremolata mixture. Grill the fish high above the coals until
just done and the flesh flakes easily with a fork. (Alternatively,
bake it in an oven preheated to 200 °C [400 °F].)
   Serve with caramelised lemons and baby potatoes.
   Serves 4.

Caramelised lemons

Halve 3 lemons or 6 limes and sprinkle the cut sides with
sugar. Grill over coals or in a nonstick pan with cut sides
facing down. Ensure the lemons don't burn.

Baby potatoes

Cook the potatoes in boiling salted water until done. Remove
the skins while hot. Sprinkle with olive oil and season with
Maldon salt and freshly ground black pepper.

Roasted cherry tomato and ricotta salad

500 g cherry tomatoes on
   the vine
6 large garlic cloves, unpeeled
45 ml (3 T) extra-virgin
   olive oil
30 ml (2 T) balsamic vinegar
5 ml (1 t) sugar
freshly ground sea salt and
   black pepper
500 g ricotta cheese
extra olive oil
fresh basil
extra balsamic vinegar

Since ricotta cheese contains very little fat it won't melt when it is fried.

Preheat the oven to 200 °C (400 °F).

Arrange the tomatoes on a baking sheet. Crush the garlic cloves with the blade of a knife and add to the tomatoes. Drizzle with the olive oil and vinegar and season with the sugar, salt and pepper. Roast the tomatoes for 10 minutes or until the skins begin to burst.

Slice the ricotta into 5 mm thick slices. Pour a little olive oil into a nonstick frying pan and fry the ricotta slices until golden on the outside. Remove from the pan and season. Arrange the tomatoes, ricotta and basil leaves on a platter. Drizzle with the pan juices, balsamic vinegar and olive oil.

Serves 4.

Grape bread

1 packet (10 g) dried yeast
   (not instant yeast)
10 ml (2 t) castor sugar
200 ml lukewarm water
125 ml (½ c) extra-virgin
   olive oil
15 ml (1 T) finely chopped
   fresh rosemary
1 garlic clove, unpeeled
   and crushed
750 ml (3 c) cake flour, sifted
2 ml (½ t) salt
500 g seedless black grapes
Maldon salt and castor sugar
   for sprinkling

Grapes and fresh rosemary add a unique flavour to this bread.

Mix the yeast and sugar with the lukewarm water, stirring until dissolved. Set aside until frothy.

Gently heat the olive oil, rosemary and garlic until fragrant. Cool, then remove the garlic.

Place the flour and salt in a large mixing bowl. Add the yeast mixture and half the infused olive oil. Mix to form a dough and knead on a floured surface for about 10 minutes. Return the dough to the bowl, add the grapes and work them into the dough. Transfer the dough to a clean bowl, oiled with the rosemary oil. Brush the top of the dough with more oil. Cover with a sheet of cling film and leave to rise until it has doubled in volume.

Brush a round loose-bottomed cake tin with the rosemary oil and press the dough into the tin. Brush the top with any remaining rosemary oil and sprinkle with a pinch of salt and castor sugar. Leave to rise for 30 minutes in a warm place.

Preheat the oven to 200 °C (400 °F). Place the cake tin on a baking sheet to catch any juices and bake the bread for 30–40 minutes until golden brown and done or until it sounds hollow when tapped underneath.

Serve lukewarm with olive oil or butter.

Makes 1 loaf.

roasted cherry tomato and ricotta salad

roasted artichoke hearts

Caramelised onion tart

1 roll bought puff pastry,
  thawed
2–3 red onions, cut
  into wedges
olive oil
white wine vinegar
sugar
salt and black pepper to taste
50 g tallegio cheese, sliced
fresh sage leaves
60 ml (4 T) crème fraîche or
  sour cream

Very more-ish.

Preheat the oven to 180 °C (350 °F). Grease a rectangular loose-bottomed pie dish with butter or margarine or spray with nonstick spray and line with the rolled pastry. Prick the crust and leave to rest in the fridge for 30 minutes.

Arrange the onions on a baking sheet and drizzle with olive oil and white wine vinegar. Sprinkle with sugar, season well and roast until the onions are caramelised and the ends slightly charred. Arrange the caramelised onions and cheese on the crust in the prepared pie dish and insert fresh sage leaves among the onions. Season well and spoon a few dollops of crème fraîche on top. Increase oven temperature to 220 °C (425 °F) and bake the tart until the pastry is done and golden brown.

Serves 4.

Roasted artichoke hearts

8 fresh artichokes
2 lemons
fresh lemon thyme
8 garlic cloves, unpeeled
30 ml (2 T) extra-virgin
  olive oil
125 ml (½ c) white wine
50 g butter
Maldon salt
freshly ground black pepper

Special vegetables such as artichoke hearts are ideal for this stylish braai.

Preheat the oven to 180 °C (350 °F).

Remove the tough outer leaves of the artichokes and cut away two-thirds of the leaves to reveal the choke in the centre. Using a teaspoon, gently scoop out the hard, spiky centre. Using a sharp knife, trim and neaten the outside. While preparing the remaining artichokes place the peeled hearts in a bowl of water to which the juice of 1 lemon has been added. Place the artichokes, lemon thyme and garlic cloves on a baking sheet. Drizzle with the olive oil and wine and add the remaining lemon, cut into pieces. Dot with knobs of butter and season well. Cover tightly with foil and roast for 45 minutes until tender.

Serves 4.

Hint
Alternatively, place the baking sheet over the coals.

Braaied baby beetroot

8 baby beetroot, scrubbed
4 garlic cloves, unpeeled
a handful of fresh thyme
30 ml (2 T) extra-virgin
  olive oil
60 ml (4 T) balsamic vinegar
salt and pepper
sugar

Fold a large sheet of heavy-duty foil in half and place on a work surface. Keep the roots of the beetroot intact and cut off the stalks 3 cm from the top. Place the beetroot, garlic and thyme in the middle of the sheet of foil. Drizzle with the oil and vinegar and season well with salt, pepper and sugar. Wrap the beetroot and other ingredients in the foil and roast over coals until the beetroot is soft and done.
  Serves 4.

Grilled vegetables with Parmesan cheese

Slice 1–2 brinjals and a few baby marrows lengthways. Grill over coals or in a well-heated griddle pan until the edges begin to blacken. Place in a dish. Slice 2 peeled garlic cloves thinly and mix with 1–2 sprigs of fresh lemon thyme and a dash or two of olive oil. Pour over the vegetables and cool to room temperature. Serve with Parmesan cheese shavings.
  Serves 4.

Summer fruit in spicy muscadel

syrup
1 bottle (750 ml) white
  muscadel
250 ml (1 c) white sugar
125 ml (½ c) honey
2 cinnamon sticks
4 cardamom pods
5 whole cloves
2 star anise
1 vanilla pod
squeeze of fresh lemon juice

selection of stone summer
  fruit, such as peaches,
  nectarines, apricots
  and plums

Make three days in advance to allow the flavours to develop.

Bring al the ingredients for the syrup to the boil in a saucepan and simmer gently.
  Place the fruit in the syrup and poach gently until just soft and easy to peel. Remove the nectarines and peaches from the syrup and leave the rest of the fruit to cool in the syrup. Peel the nectarines and peaches and return to the syrup. Allow to stand for 2–3 days to allow the fruit to absorb the syrup.
  Serves 4.

Strawberry ice cream with nougat

Bring 500 ml (2 c) full-cream milk, 500 ml (2 c) cream and a vanilla pod, slit open, to the boil. Remove from heat and allow to stand for 10 minutes to allow the vanilla to infuse the milk. Beat together 8 egg yolks and 150 g castor sugar until pale. Slowly add the milk mixture to the egg mixture, stirring continuously. Return to the heat and heat very gently, stirring continuously, until the mixture thickens slightly and coats the back of a wooden spoon. Cool completely. Turn the mixture into an ice-cream maker and freeze according to the manufacturer's instructions. (Alternatively, pour into a metal bowl, freeze and beat a few times to break up the ice crystals.)

Cut 600 g ripe strawberries and 2 nougat bars into small cubes. Thaw ice cream slightly and fold in the strawberries and nougat. Freeze once more. Serve in ice cream cones.

Makes about 2 litres.

strawberry ice cream with nougat

holiday
fare

Holidays are meant for resting, for visiting friends you haven't seen for ages, lazy walks on the beach and long leisurely meals. It's time to take it easy, relax and indulge in delicious food. Nibble bread and cheese and sip wine in true Mediterranean style; eat fish fresh from the sea and imagine yourself holidaying on a Greek island.

holiday entertaining

Invite friends and prepare hassle-free food to get you in the holiday mood.

platter with cold meats, cheese and fruit

Menu
Lemonade
Platter of cold meats,
  cheese and fruit

Barbecue chicken
Spicy pork chops
Spinach, brinjal and
  walnut salad
Butter bean salad
Herbed flat bread with
  Parmesan shavings

Mini strawberry pavlovas
  with ice cream

Lemonade

680 ml (2¾ c) sugar
1,125 litres (4½ c) cold water
560 ml (2¼ c) lemon juice
ice cubes
1 lime, sliced

Slowly heat the sugar and cold water until all the sugar has dissolved. Stir occasionally. Bring to the boil, cover the sauce-pan and boil for 3 minutes. Remove from the heat and stir in the lemon juice. Chill. Add the ice and lime slices. Serve diluted.
    Makes about 2 litres.

Platter of cold meats, cheese and fruit

selection of cold meats such
  as thin slices of smoked
  turkey, smoked pepper ham
  and spiced beef
cheeses such as Camembert,
  Emmenthal and Dutch
  boeren cheese
fruit in season such as
  pawpaw, melon, peaches
  and prickly pears, sliced
  into thin wedges
fresh mint

Arrange the meat, cheese and fruit on an attractive platter and scatter mint on top. Keep chilled until ready to serve (do not assemble too long in advance).

Barbecue chicken

sauce
30 ml (2 T) olive oil
1 large onion, finely chopped
2 cans (200 g each) chopped
  tomatoes
2 cans (65 g each) tomato
  paste
250 ml (1 c) red wine vinegar
125 ml (½ c) light brown sugar
60 ml (4 T) Worcester sauce
80 ml (⅓ c) brown sugar
4 ml (¾ t) cayenne pepper

8 chicken pieces
salt

Heat the oil and sauté the onion until soft. Stir in the chopped tomatoes and tomato paste and add the remaining ingredients, except the chicken and salt. Heat slowly until the mixture comes to the boil. Reduce the heat and simmer uncovered for about 45 minutes. Set aside 375 ml (1½ c) of the sauce for serving with the chicken.

Lightly salt the chicken and brush with a little of the remaining sauce. Braai high above the coals, basting frequently with the sauce. Cook the chicken until done but still juicy. Serve with the reserved sauce.

Serves 6–8.

Spicy pork chops

spice mixture
7 ml (1½ t) paprika
15 ml (1 T) ground coriander
15 ml (1 T) finely grated
  lemon rind
15 ml (1 T) dried marjoram
1 clove garlic, crushed
5 ml (1 t) salt
4 ml (¾ t) freshly ground
  black pepper
2 ml (½ t) ground cumin
1 ml (¼ t) caraway seeds
1 ml (¼ t) ground cinnamon
olive oil

8 thick pork chops or boned
  pork neck

Mix all the ingredients for the spice mixture, adding a little olive oil to moisten. Rub the mixture into both sides of the pork chops, pressing it into the meat. Chill for 20 minutes. Braai the chops over medium coals until done but still juicy.

Serves 6–8

Butter bean salad

salad dressing
50 ml olive oil
15 ml (1 T) red wine vinegar
45 ml (3 T) finely chopped
  fresh parsley
salt and freshly ground
  black pepper

2 cans (410 g each) butter
  beans, drained
2 tomatoes, chopped
50 g (½ packet) black or green
  olives, stoned and coarsely
  chopped

Make a dressing by whisking the olive oil and vinegar together. Add the parsley and season with salt and pepper. Combine the butter beans, tomatoes and olives. Moisten with the salad dressing and mix lightly.
  Serves 6–8.

Herbed flat bread with Parmesan shavings

1 kg prepared bread dough
30 ml (2 T) olive oil
15 ml (1 T) finely chopped
  fresh parsley
30 ml (2 T) coarse salt
30 ml (2 T) Parmesan
  shavings

Serve this bread with tomato salsa, if preferred.

Preheat the oven to 190 °C (375 °F) and grease a large baking sheet lightly with butter or margarine or spray with nonstick spray.
  Knock down the dough and shape into a flat round. Mix the olive oil and parsley and brush the surface of the dough with the mixture. Sprinkle with coarse salt and leave the dough to rise slightly. Bake for 20–30 minutes or until done. Sprinkle with Parmesan cheese shavings as soon as the bread comes out of the oven.
  Serve lukewarm.
  Serves 6.

Tomato salsa

Mix 3 chopped tomatoes with 15 ml (1 T) chopped fresh coriander leaves and season with a dash of balsamic vinegar, salt and freshly ground black pepper.

herbed flat bread with Parmesan shavings and tomato salsa

mini strawberry pavlovas

Spinach, brinjal and walnut salad

1 medium brinjal, cubed
salt
30 ml (2 T) olive oil
175 g shoulder bacon,
  chopped
100 g button mushrooms,
  quartered
200 g baby spinach leaves,
  rinsed and shredded
75 g (¾ packet) walnuts,
  chopped

dressing
60 ml (4 T) olive oil
30 ml (2 T) balsamic vinegar

The walnuts and bacon add a wonderful flavour and texture to this salad. Replace the brinjal with butternut if desired.

Sprinkle the brinjal cubes with salt and leave to sweat for about 15 minutes. Rinse and pat dry. Heat the olive oil in a heavy-based pan and fry the brinjal cubes over medium heat until cooked and lightly browned. Remove from the pan. In the same pan, fry the bacon and mushrooms until done. Mix with the fried brinjal cubes, spinach and walnuts.

Make the dressing by whisking the olive oil and balsamic vinegar together and sprinkle over the salad.

Serves 6–8.

Mini strawberry pavlovas

4 extra-large egg whites
pinch salt
250 ml (1 c) castor sugar
30 ml (2 T) cornflour
15 ml (1 T) white wine vinegar
6–8 scoops chocolate-mint
  ice-cream

strawberry topping
500 g fresh strawberries,
  hulled and cleaned
45 ml (3 T) icing sugar
15 ml (1 T) balsamic vinegar
kebab skewers

Preheat the oven to 180 °C (350 °F) and line 2 baking sheets with baking paper. Dust with cornflour.

Whisk the egg whites and salt until soft peaks form. Add the castor sugar a little at a time, beating until the egg whites are stiff and shiny. Fold in cornflour and vinegar. Drop large spoonfuls of the meringue on the prepared baking sheets, spreading each out to form a fairly flat round. Make a hollow in the centre of each round. Bake the meringues for 5 minutes, reduce the oven temperature to 110 °C (200 °F) and bake for another 1¼ hours. Cool in the oven and store the meringues in airtight containers.

Process half the strawberries, 25 ml (5 t) of the icing sugar, and the vinegar in a food processor until chunky. Chill until needed. Thread the remaining strawberries onto kebab skewers, dust with the remaining icing sugar and braai over medium coals until they just begin to brown.

To serve: Place a meringue on a side plate, spoon a scoop of chocolate-mint ice cream into the hollow and top with the strawberry sauce. Serve with the grilled strawberries.

Serves 6–8.

Mediterranean island food

Do things the Mediterranean way: nibble on foods served at room temperature and eat fish fresh from the sea.

Marinated seafood

1 kg frozen seafood mixture
cake flour
salt and freshly ground
  black pepper
125 ml (½ c) oil
4 bay leaves
1 lemon, sliced
6 sprigs parsley
2 large onions, sliced
  into rings
6 garlic cloves, peeled
2 large carrots, scraped and
  thinly sliced
5 ml (1 t) paprika
180 ml (¾ c) grape or white
  wine vinegar
180 ml (¾ c) white wine
100 ml water

Marinate in the fridge for 2 days.

Pour boiling water over the seafood mix and leave to thaw. Pat dry and roll in cake flour seasoned generously with salt and freshly ground black pepper. Heat some of the oil and fry the seafood rapidly until just tender and done, about 2–3 minutes. Transfer to an earthenware dish. Scatter the bay leaves, lemon slices and parsley on top and chill.

Heat the remaining oil and sauté the onions, garlic and carrots until tender. Add the paprika, vinegar and wine and simmer for 5 minutes. Remove from the heat, add the water and leave to cool. Pour over the seafood and marinate in the fridge for at least 24 hours. Serve at room temperature.
  Serves 6.

marinated seafood

fried fish with Mediterranean salsa and tzatsiki

Fried fish with Mediterranean salsa

any fresh white fish such
  as blacktail, steenbras or
  stumpnose
salt and pepper
cake flour
oil

Werner van der Walt, head chef of Club Mykonos near Lange-baan on the West Coast, prepared this tasty fish for us. It's cooked in a frying pan and served with salsa.

Gut the fish and remove the gills and scales. Season the fish well with salt and pepper and roll in flour to coat.

Heat enough oil in a large shallow pan and fry the fish for about 10 minutes on each side or until golden brown and done but still juicy. Insert a knife into the flesh on the back of the fish – if it's no longer glassy and it flakes easily, the fish is done.

Serve immediately with salsa and roasted vegetables in pittas, and with tzatsiki (chopped cucumber and natural yoghurt).

Serves 4–6.

Salsa

125 ml (½ c) peeled, seeded
  and chopped tomatoes
15 ml (1 T) chopped
  fresh fennel
15 ml (1 T) chopped
  fresh basil
⅓ medium red sweet pepper,
  seeded and diced
⅓ medium yellow sweet
  pepper, seeded and diced
60 ml (4 T) chopped chives
30 ml (2 T) stoned black
  olives, finely chopped
70 ml verjuice
30 ml (2 T) verjuice syrup
  (optional)
salt and black pepper

Blend all the ingredients for the salsa and serve with the fish.

Makes about 300 ml.

Roasted vegetables with aniseed

Halve baby marrows lengthways. Slice seeded red and yellow sweet peppers and a small brinjal into long strips. Arrange in a roasting pan along with 6 button mushrooms and drizzle with olive oil. Sprinkle with coarsely ground aniseed, black pepper, salt and coriander and roast at 190 °C (375 °F) until the vegetables are done and starting to brown. Serve in pittas with the fish.

Serves 4–6.

Chicken in white wine

30 ml (2 T) olive oil
1 onion, chopped
3 large garlic cloves, crushed
1 whole chicken, cut
  into pieces
salt and freshly ground
  black pepper
sprigs of fresh herbs such
  as thyme, rosemary
  and oregano
250 ml (1 c) white wine
juice of ½ lemon
10 green olives

The wine, lemon and herbs impart a wonderful flavour to this chicken dish.

Heat the oil in a large pan and fry the onion and garlic until soft. Add the chicken pieces, season with salt and pepper and brown. Add the herbs and white wine. Bring to the boil, reduce the heat and simmer until the chicken is tender and done. Add the lemon juice and green olives and leave the chicken to cool in the liquid.

Reheat just before serving or serve cold with a green salad, olive oil and bread on the side.

Serves 4.

Brinjal and tomato salad

2–3 brinjals, cubed
salt
100 ml olive oil
1 onion, sliced into rings
1 bunch celery with leaves,
  finely chopped
500 g ripe plum tomatoes,
  skinned and chopped
125 ml (½ c) red wine vinegar
15 ml (1 T) white sugar
15 ml (1 T) capers
salt and freshly ground
  black pepper
30 ml (2 T) finely chopped
  fresh parsley

Make this salad in advance and keep it in the fridge.

Sprinkle the brinjal cubes with salt and leave to drain. Rinse and pat dry with paper towels.

Heat 30 ml (2 T) of the olive oil and sauté the onion until tender. Add the celery and sauté for another 5 minutes. Add the tomatoes and simmer for 5 minutes. Add the vinegar, sugar and capers. Simmer until the tomatoes have disintegrated and a fragrant sauce has formed.

Meanwhile, fry the brinjal cubes in the remaining oil until browned all over and done. Drain on paper towels. Mix the brinjal cubes with the tomato sauce. Season to taste with salt, pepper and extra sugar to taste. Stir in the parsley. Cool, preferably not in the fridge. Refrigerate for about 2 days to allow the flavours to develop.

Serves 4–6.

Almond cake

125 ml (½ c) almond slivers
125 ml (½ c) ground almonds
125 ml (½ c) mealie meal
125 ml (½ c) cake flour
22 ml (1½ T) cornflour
5 ml (1 t) baking powder
2 ml (½ t) salt
30 ml (2 T) butter
30 ml (2 T) sugar
180 g butter
250 ml (1 c) sugar
3 extra-large eggs
45 ml (3 T) fresh orange juice
2 ml (½ t) vanilla essence
grated rind of ½ lemon

A moist cake made with mealie meal and almonds.

Preheat the oven to 160 °C (325 °F). Toast the slivered almonds on a baking sheet in the oven until golden brown. Leave to cool. Combine the ground almonds and dry ingredients. Melt the 30 ml (2 T) butter and use to grease the base and sides of a 20 cm diameter cake tin. Sprinkle with the 30 ml (2 T) sugar and the slivered almonds.

Cream the 180 g butter and 250 ml (1 c) sugar together in a food processor until creamy. Add the eggs one by one, mixing well after each addition. Add the orange juice, vanilla essence and lemon rind. Add the flour mixture and process until just mixed.

Turn the batter into the prepared tin, spreading it out evenly. Bake for about 45 minutes or until a skewer inserted into the centre of the cake comes out clean. Cool for 15 minutes before turning it out onto a wire rack and leaving to cool. Serve with tea.

Makes 1 large cake.

almond cake

hassle-free holiday food

quick pasta

Egg fry-up
Quick pasta
Quick fish pie
Greek lamb pizza
Thai chicken burgers
Thai chicken curry
Fruity chicken salad
  with green pepper and
  coriander
Easy sweetcorn tart
Spanish rice with chorizo
  sausages
Hot potato salad with tuna
  and pesto dressing
Spicy potatoes
Chicken noodle salad
Quick ginger beer
Frozen yoghurt
Caramel rice pudding
Microwaved lemon tart

Egg fry-up

15 ml (1 T) olive oil
250 g cooked baby potatoes,
  cut into chunks
2 ml (½ t) chilli flakes
1 garlic clove, finely chopped
salt and freshly ground black
  pepper
200 g cherry tomatoes,
  halved
4 extra-large eggs
handful fresh coriander or
  parsley, coarsely chopped

Perfect for a brunch or light supper.

Heat the oil in a heavy-based frying pan and stir-fry the potatoes until they just begin to brown. Sprinkle with the chilli flakes and garlic and stir to mix. Season well with salt and pepper. Add the tomatoes and stir-fry for about 3 minutes. Make 4 hollows in the mixture and break an egg into each. Season with salt and pepper once more, cover and heat until the eggs are cooked to taste. Scatter the coriander or parsley on top and serve immediately.
Serves 2–4.

Quick pasta

30 ml (2 T) olive oil
2 red sweet peppers, seeded
  and cut into strips
1 large onion, sliced
2 garlic cloves, finely
  chopped
2 cans (400 g each) chopped
  tomatoes
salt and freshly ground
  black pepper
300 g penne or rigatoni pasta
100 g shoulder bacon (fat
  removed), chopped
250 ml (1 c) breadcrumbs
30 ml (2 T) finely chopped
  fresh rosemary
125 ml (½ c) grated
  mozzarella cheese

Preheat the oven to 200 °C (400 °F) and grease a 25 cm x 30 cm ovenproof dish with olive oil or spray with nonstick spray.

Heat the olive oil in a pan and slowly sauté the sweet peppers and onion. Add the garlic and sauté for 1 minute. Add the tomatoes and bring to the boil. Season well with salt and freshly ground black pepper.

Meanwhile, cook the pasta in a pot of rapidly boiling salted water until tender but still al dente (firm to the bite). Fry the bacon until crisp (don't add any extra fat), add to the pasta sauce and stir. Combine the pasta and sauce and transfer to the prepared dish. Mix the breadcrumbs, rosemary and mozzarella cheese and sprinkle over the pasta. Bake for 20 minutes or until the breadcrumbs are golden.

Serves 4.

Variation
Replace the bacon with olives for a vegetarian meal.

Hint
Rather steam vegetables than boil them – they retain their colour, texture and nutrients better.

Quick fish pie

250 g frozen haddock fillets
250 ml (1 c) fat-free milk
250 ml (1 c) frozen peas
10 ml (2 t) butter or margarine
15 ml (1 T) cake flour
90 ml (6 T) smooth cottage
  cheese
400 g mashed potatoes,
  made without butter

Preheat the oven to 190 °C (375 °F) and grease a 20 cm x 22 cm ovenproof dish lightly with olive oil, or spray with nonstick spray.

Place the haddock and milk in a saucepan, bring to the boil and simmer until the fish is done and flakes easily with a fork. Remove the fish from the pan and leave to cool. Reserve the milk. Flake the fish and place in the prepared dish, along with the peas.

Melt the butter or margarine and stir in the flour, heating it until cooked (about 1 minute). Gradually add the reserved milk. Stirring continuously, heat until the mixture comes to the boil and thickens to form a smooth sauce. Remove from the heat and stir in the cottage cheese. Pour the sauce over the fish and mix. Spoon the mashed potato on top and bake for 25–30 minutes or until the potato is golden brown.

Serves 4.

Greek lamb pizza

marinated lamb
350 g lamb, cut into strips
5 ml (1 t) salt
15 ml (1 T) oregano
10 ml (2 t) soy sauce
45 ml (3 T) lemon juice
1 garlic clove, crushed
45 ml (3 T) olive oil

base
375 ml (1½ c) warm water
30 ml (2 T) instant yeast
4 x 250 ml (4 c) cake flour
freshly ground black pepper
3 ml (generous ½ t) each
 basil, thyme, oregano, garlic
 salt, onion salt and chervil

to assemble
olive oil for frying
1 onion, thinly sliced
80 g mushrooms, sliced
150 g sun-dried tomatoes in
 vinaigrette, chopped
100 g calamata olives, pitted
375 ml (1½ c) grated
 mozzarella cheese
375 ml (1½ c) crumbled feta
 cheese

Use frozen pizza bases if you run out of time.

Place the meat strips in a glass dish. Mix the remaining ingredients for the marinade, pour over the meat and mix well. Cover and marinate for 2 hours.

Meanwhile, pour the warm water into a mixing bowl, sprinkle the instant yeast on top and leave to stand for 5 minutes. Add 500 ml (2 c) of the flour, along with the pepper and herbs. Stir to form a smooth batter. Add another 250 ml (1 c) of flour. Stir until the mixture forms a ball. Add more flour to make a smooth dough (it mustn't be sticky). Knead the dough for about 5 minutes or until elastic, cover and leave to rise in a warm place until doubled in volume. Knock down, divide the dough in half and roll each half out into a 28 cm round. Leave for 15 minutes to rise again.

To assemble: Drain the meat strips and fry them rapidly in a little olive oil until just done. Remove from the pan and leave to cool. Preheat the oven to 220 °C (425 °F) and grease 2 pizza pans or baking sheets with oil. Place the dough rounds on top and, working from the centre of the circle outwards, press the dough so it covers the entire pan or sheet. Arrange the meat on top, followed by the onion, mushrooms, sun-dried tomatoes, olives and cheese. Bake for 15–20 minutes or until the bases are done and the cheese has melted.

Makes 2 medium pizzas.

Thai chicken burgers

30 ml (2 T) Thai spice
4 boned chicken breasts
oil
4 hamburger rolls
butter or margarine (optional)
30 ml (2 T) sweet chilli sauce
45 ml (3 T) coconut milk
¼ English cucumber
bean sprouts

Make these instead of ordinary hamburgers. The kids will love them!

Rub the spice into the chicken pieces. Fry the chicken in a little heated oil in a griddle pan until just done and still juicy. Halve the rolls, but don't slice all the way through. Spread with butter or margarine if desired. Place a chicken breast inside each roll. Blend the chilli sauce and coconut milk and spoon a little of the mixture over each chicken breast. Slice the cucumber into thin strips using a potato peeler and stack on top of the meat. Garnish with bean sprouts.

Serves 4.

greek lamb pizza

Thai chicken curry

sauce
30 ml (2 T) Thai green
 curry paste
1 can (400 g) coconut milk
juice of ½ lemon
a few curry leaves
a few fresh basil leaves
1–2 drops fish sauce
30 ml (2 T) chopped fresh
 coriander leaves
1–2 drops soy sauce

chicken
2–4 boned chicken breasts,
 cut into strips
olive oil
400 g stir-fry vegetables
 such as carrots, baby
 marrows, spinach, chives,
 mushrooms, butternut and
 baby mealies
chopped cashew nuts
fresh coriander leaves

You can prepare this curry without the vegetables too.

Mix all the sauce ingredients in a saucepan, bring to the boil
and simmer until fragrant. Set aside.

Stir-fry the chicken strips in olive oil until just done. Add the
vegetables and stir-fry for 1–2 minutes. Add the Thai sauce
and simmer for 5 minutes. Serve with sticky rice or vermicelli-
noodles. Sprinkle with cashew nuts and coriander leaves.

Serves 4.

Thai chicken curry

Fruity chicken salad with green pepper and coriander

800 g leftover, cooked
  chicken, cut into pieces
2 nectarines, and 2 cling
  peaches, stoned and sliced
  into pieces
½ small melon, seeded,
  peeled and cubed
1 can mangoes, drained and
  cut into pieces
2 green chillies, chopped
25 g coriander, chopped

salad dressing
30 ml (2 T) mayonnaise
60 ml (4 T) sour cream
salt and ground black pepper
15 ml (1 T) cumin seeds,
  toasted

We made our salad with nectarines, cling peaches and melon but you can also use mangoes, pears, figs or any other fruit of your choice.

Combine the chicken pieces, fruit, chillies and coriander. Make a dressing by beating together the mayonnaise and sour cream and use to moisten the salad. Season well with salt and freshly ground black pepper and sprinkle with the toasted cumin seeds.
  Serves 6.

Easy sweetcorn tart

3 rashers bacon, chopped
2 tomatoes, peeled, seeded
  and chopped
1 can (310 g) whole-kernel
  corn, drained
10 ml (2 t) curry powder
250 ml (1 c) grated
  Cheddar cheese
4 extra-large eggs, beaten

Keep a can of whole-kernel corn on hand to make this delicious tart.

Preheat the oven to 180 °C (350 °F) and grease a 24 cm diameter pie dish with butter or margarine or spray with nonstick spray.
  Fry the bacon in a pan until done. Mix with the remaining ingredients and turn the mixture into the prepared dish. Bake for 30 minutes or until just firm.
  Serve with a salad.
  Serves 4.

Spanish rice with chorizo sausages

250 ml (1 c) uncooked rice
45 ml (3 T) oil
1 onion, chopped
1 garlic clove, crushed
1 green sweet pepper, seeded
  and diced
1 red sweet pepper, seeded
  and diced
1 can (400 g) chopped
  tomatoes
2 ml (½ t) ground cumin
3 ml (generous ½ t) dried
  basil
salt and black pepper to taste
2 chorizo sausages

Wrap the rice mixture in a tortilla and serve as hand food.

Cook the rice according to the packet instructions. Heat the oil in a large pan and stir-fry the onion, garlic and sweet peppers until just done. Add the tomatoes, seasoning and rice and heat until the mixture is thick and fragrant. Fry the sausages until done, slice and add to the rice mixture. Serve with a salad.
  Serves 4–6.

Hot potato salad with tuna and pesto dressing

650 g baby potatoes,
  scrubbed and halved
200 g young green
  beans, halved
few handfuls baby
  spinach leaves
30 ml (2 T) basil pesto
60 ml (¼ c) olive oil
8 cherry tomatoes, halved
1 can (175 g) tuna, in oil
  or brine

Bring the potatoes to the boil in salted water and cook until tender. Add the beans and boil for another 3 minutes until the beans are just tender. Drain and transfer to a salad bowl. Add the spinach leaves to the hot vegetables and leave them to wilt slightly.

Make a dressing by mixing the pesto and oil together and set aside. Add the tomatoes and tuna to the vegetables and mix gently. Pour the salad dressing over and serve immediately.

Serves 4–6.

Spicy potatoes

oil
4 cooked potatoes,
  thickly sliced
5–10 ml (1–2 t) Cajun spice
  or a mixture of 5 ml (1 t)
  coriander, 2 ml (½ t) cumin
  and 2–3 ml (½ to generous
  ½ t) cayenne pepper
5 ml (1 t) cumin seeds
20 ml (4 t) sesame seeds
½ medium onion, chopped
½ ripe, but firm, avocado,
  peeled and roughly
  chopped
1 tomato, finely chopped
salt and pepper
lemon juice
4 tortillas

A lovely side dish made with leftover potatoes. Otherwise, wrap in tortillas and serve as a light meal.

Heat the oil in a pan. Roll the potato slices in the spices and seeds and stir-fry in oil until crisp on the outside.

Mix the onion, avocado and tomato. Season with salt, pepper and lemon juice. Divide the mixture between 4 tortillas, top the potatoes with a generous spoonful of the avocado mixture and roll up. Serve with sour cream or mayonnaise, sweet chilli sauce and fresh coriander.

Serves 4.

Chicken noodle salad

3 packets instant noodles
450 g cooked leftover
  chicken, cut into pieces
2 bunches chives, chopped
1 red chilli, seeded and
  finely chopped
20 g fresh coriander,
  coarsely chopped
45 ml (3 T) sesame
  seeds, toasted
100 ml olive oil
60 ml (4 T) lemon juice
3 large garlic cloves, crushed
15 ml (1 T) fresh ginger,
  peeled and grated
15 ml (1 T) castor sugar

A dish with a Thai twist which makes a light meal.

In a large dish, soak the noodles in boiling water for 5 minutes. Drain and rinse under cold water. Place the noodles in a mixing bowl along with the chicken, chives, chilli, coriander and sesame seeds. Beat the remaining ingredients together and pour over the salad. Mix well and serve as a light meal.
Serves 6–8.

Quick ginger beer

1 kg (4 c) sugar
15 ml (1 T) Jamaica ginger
  (in bottle)
10 x 250 ml (10 c) warm water
1 packet (15 g) instant yeast

Mix the ingredients together, stirring until the sugar has dissolved. Leave for 4 hours and skim off the foam. Bottle and cork.
  Makes about 3 litres ginger beer.

Frozen yoghurt

Process 500 g frozen berries, 400 g fat-free plain yoghurt, 100 ml fresh orange juice and 15 ml (1 T) icing sugar in a food processor until well-blended. Serve for breakfast or as an in-between treat.
  Serves 3–4.

Caramel rice pudding

750 ml (3 c) milk
125 ml (½ c) uncooked rice
125 ml (½ c) seedless raisins
60 ml (4 T) coconut
15 ml (1 T) margarine
1 packet instant caramel
  pudding
500 ml (2 c) cold milk
5 ml (1 t) ground cinnamon
3 ml (generous ½ t) nutmeg
5 ml (1 t) caramel essence

Bring the 750 ml (3 c) milk to the boil and stir in the rice, raisins and coconut. Cover and simmer, stirring occasionally, until all the milk has been absorbed. Stir in the margarine. Mix the instant pudding powder with 500 ml (2 c) cold milk, add the cinnamon, nutmeg and caramel essence and whisk until the mixture begins to thicken. Stir into the cooked rice mixture. Serve immediately or chill.
Serves 6.

Instant puddings

- Spoon canned fruit, fresh strawberries or berries into individual bowls and top with custard and a sprinkling of brown sugar. Heat under the grill until the sugar is slightly caramelised.
- Process strawberries or other berries with icing sugar in a food processor. Serve in tall glasses, layered alternately with canned peaches and topped with a scoop of ice cream.
- Make very strong coffee with instant coffee granules. Spoon a few scoops of ice cream into tall glasses and pour a little of the coffee over. Serve with finger biscuits.
- Sprinkle mixed berries with plenty of brown sugar and add a few tots of brandy. Bring to the boil and simmer until the liquid is syrupy. Serve with whipped cream or ice cream.

Microwaved lemon tart

crust
1 packet (200 g) Tennis
  biscuits, crushed
100 g butter or margarine,
  melted

filling
2 extra-large eggs
5 ml (1 t) vanilla essence
100 ml lemon juice
300 ml castor sugar
2 ml (½ t) salt
50 ml cornflour
50 ml custard powder
400 ml milk

Crust: Mix the crushed biscuits and melted butter. Line a 24 cm diameter pie dish with the mixture and chill.

Filling: Beat the eggs, vanilla essence and lemon juice together. Sift the castor sugar, salt, cornflour and custard powder on top and stir to form a paste. In a glass bowl microwave the milk for 2 minutes at 100 per cent power. Add a little of the hot milk to the egg mixture and stir well. Return everything to the glass bowl with the rest of the milk. Microwave for 5–6 minutes at 100 per cent power until thick and done, beating with a wire whisk at 2-minute intervals. Pour the mixture into the prepared crust, spreading it out evenly. Chill until firm. Decorate with lemon strips.

Makes 1 medium tart.

microwave lemon tart

index